D1736092

HUNT
OR
BE HUNTED

HOW ANYONE
CAN DEVELOP GRIT
AND LEAD LIKE A LEGEND

LARA **JONES**

Scan the QR code to get a
sneak peek into your grit strength.
See quick insights in just minutes.

www.larajones.com

ISBN: 9798863634746

CONTENTS

Chapter 7: Reframe Thinking:
The "R" in the Global G.R.I.T. System™   91

Chapter 8: Impact Others:
The "I" in the Global G.R.I.T. System™   109

Chapter 9: Take Responsibility:
The "T" in the Global G.R.I.T. System™   122

CHAPTER 1

Welcome to
the Hunt

---

*"The greatest danger for most of us is not
that our aim is too high and we miss it,
but that it is too low and wo reach it."*

Michelangelo

Hunt or Be Hunted

Picture the Serengeti. A lioness is nestled in the long wavering grass, watching and waiting for the right time to strike. She studies her target, watching every move, sometimes waiting hours for the right moment. Any slight movement and her chance to capture her prey is gone. Meanwhile, the prey, oblivious to the lioness waiting only feet away, watching silently, thinks they are safe, maybe because they are in a group, maybe because they can't hear or see their hunter, maybe because they haven't seen their predator in that area that day. What do you think will happen next? The lioness attacks and does not go hungry.

So what's the major difference between the hunter and the hunted?

Grit.

What do I mean by that? Since she was young, the lioness has learned the right way to hunt. She has learned from failed attempts to hunt her prey, and has learned patience. Lions can sometimes wait many hours before they make their move, learning to be very quiet and still during the process. And that's just it, there is a process and the lioness knows this. She can't just ambush at the wrong moment, she will go hungry if she does. She also knows that this isn't just about her and her needs. Her process is not just for her. It's for her family. She has a responsibility to feed her cubs, her pride.

The same can be said in our world, outside of the Serengeti. We can learn a great deal from the wild, because 10,000 years ago it wasn't much different for us.

There are two types of people in this world. The hunters and the hunted. Thousands of years ago, in order to survive, we had to hunt. That meant constantly moving around to find food and catch prey, using the right side of our brain to be imaginative to create different types of tools to use, using the left side of our brain to think differently and strategize how to use the tools we created. We had to build shelter to protect us from the climate and other predators; we used methods that were tried and tested, and learned from each other. We were constantly hunting and if you didn't, guess what? You were being hunted.

Our biggest threat to humanity back then and the most common cause of death was being eaten. The same is happening in today's world, yet we can't physically see it. We are being metaphorically "eaten" every day we don't hunt, and our competitors get one step ahead of us. But this is where many will go wrong. They focus on competition, rather than focusing on themselves and asking, "Why do I do what I do?" and "Why do I help who I help?" In other words: What's the bigger "why"?

Once you understand that, it doesn't matter about the competition or what anyone else is doing, because you so passionately believe in what you do, why you do it, and how you impact others. You don't want anyone to miss out on what you offer or what you can do to impact them.

As a society, we have slowly become softer in our approach and expect much to be done for us. What do you think would have happened to our species if our ancestors took that approach 10,000 years ago? Would we exist today? The answer is no. We are constantly evolving and developing new technology and tools to help our humanity, just like our ancestors created tools to help them strategize and hunt more effectively. They became smarter. They had to evolve and evolve fast, and continue to "hunt" and become better at their hunting skills in order to survive. If we don't constantly evolve and stay on top of our game, we will lose, fail, and fall behind. Hence the phrase: "hunt or be hunted."

So why is it that some will find that grit and others won't? Why do some hunt and many are being hunted? Are they even aware they are being hunted? Probably not. And therein lies the problem. Awareness. Lack of awareness of themselves, lack of awareness of others, lack of awareness of the solutions to the problems they may face, daily, as a result of focusing on external factors rather than focusing on what they can control.

Grit is Within Your Control

I had the pleasure of sitting down with my friend Bruce Gradowski, former NFL quarterback for the St. Louis Rams, Cleveland Browns, Tampa Bay Buccaneers, Oakland Raiders, Cincinnati Bengals, and Pittsburgh Steelers and now currently coaching in the XFL as offensive coordinator for the St. Louis Battlehawks. In our interview, Bruce said something that really rang true: Grit is within your control. Bruce regularly tells his team that there are three areas that they should focus on and control:

1. Attitude
2. Preparation
3. Effort

All three of these are what lead to grit. Bruce says he would take a player with grit over a player that has talent, because he knows those players will work hard and be a good teammate. Just because you have talent doesn't mean you have grit.

The History of Grit

Why are lions the "king of the jungle"? They aren't the biggest, they aren't the fastest, so why are they the king of the jungle? Because they believe it. And they make every animal around them believe it too. This is the difference in mindset between a hunter and the hunted. In life, we all find ourselves in different roles, and we define ourselves by the title we are given. Mother, father, brother, sister, CEO, COO, CFO, SVP, VP, and the list goes on. But the titles don't truly matter. What really makes the difference in leadership is the belief you have in yourself and the belief others have in you. Much like the lion. To be the hunter you don't have to be the loudest, the strongest, or the fastest, but you do have to have the belief, courage, and discipline to push harder when everyone else is giving up.

The hunters represent those who take initiative, set goals, and actively pursue what they want. They are driven, determined, and willing to take risks to achieve their objectives. On the other hand, the hunted symbolize those who are more passive or reactive in their approach. They may find themselves constantly reacting to circumstances, avoiding risks, or being pursued by challenges or obstacles. They may feel more vulnerable or at the mercy of external factors.

How "Hunters" View the World

Ask yourself: What is our biggest currency? Money? In the context of human history, no. It didn't exist 10,000 years ago. Our biggest currency is time and relationships. We cannot get time back, we cannot create more, and we need others around us to help us gain strength. We all have a set amount of time on this planet, and so we should use it wisely. On the flip side, what do we earn by spending our currency of time? It's not objects or things, but instead our compensation is trust and building our network and relationships. Chris Gardner (inspiration for the 2006 movie *Pursuit of Happyness*) points out, "My net worth is not my self-worth." Take what Chris says here and apply this principle to grit. Having grit and following the process means your self-worth will never fluctuate, unlike your net worth. Hunters don't chase money. They focus on time. How and when they use it, and who they choose to spend time with.

In everything, there is an average. A center on the bell curve. To the left of center reside those who are doing less than average and to the right are those who are exceeding expectations and doing far more than the average human being. The right side is where you learn and grow as a hunter. That is where you win and keep on winning. That is where you realize the rewards for the work you're putting in. You aren't the average on that bell curve. You know why? Because you made a choice to learn about grit and how you can develop it. You are open to adopting the system and applying it in every aspect of your life. You will fall behind if you are "normal." It is the "extraordinary" who excel. And you are extraordinary because you already have adopted a growth mindset by reading this book, and are open to learning whether you're a seasoned leader, a new leader, an aspiring leader, or any leader in between. This book will change the way you lead, the way you think, and how you impact others. It will teach you the process of grit, as a system, to enhance your performance and effectiveness at work, with your fellow leaders, team members, and in your relationships outside of the workplace. So when we look at the common denominators between every successful person in the world, what are they? Grit and discipline.

Grit is Discipline

Bruce Gradowski defines grit as discipline in defining moments. In other words, doing something you don't want to do but you know you have to. He provides the example of getting up straight away when the alarm goes off, instead of hitting the snooze button. It's easy to hit the snooze button, but what is that really going to do for you? I agree with Bruce one hundred percent. You have to get up, show up, and give everything you can in that moment as you are the one who has to look yourself in the mirror and be okay with the effort you gave. Only you are going to know if you gave it your all or not.

So why is it so difficult to first, start and then, continue? Discipline is instrumental to achieve goals and those who master discipline are usually more successful.[1] Nick Saban (current head football coach of the University of Alabama) supports this notion with his idea of discipline being important not just with the players, but also the coaching team. Nick Saban says that nobody is entitled to a position, they earn that position by showing the capability and ability to do it on a consistent basis.[2] *Consistent* being the operative word here. That's what discipline provides. A code of behavior. Standards which are upheld and maintained. How do we achieve that? By developing good habits. Discipline is a word that many fear, but should not. The very sound of that word may cause anxiety and may send chills down some people's spines.[3] Why? Perhaps it is due to a negative connotation attached to that word from childhood. Many people associate discipline with punishment, which makes sense, because the word can mean "to punish." However, to fully embrace discipline, you need to have a positive association with the word. A human being is far more likely to succeed when positive emotions are attributed to an action versus negative ones.[4]

We as human beings tend to believe the negative (it is evolution and part of our survival) over the positive in relation to a word that has previously been identified as a threat of some kind.[5] Discipline is associated with the words "punish" and "penalize," so the very nature of hearing the word "discipline" immediately creates barriers. However, discipline is also associated with training and developing—two words that are seen in a positive light for many.

What if every action we take, owing to discipline, resulted in outstanding performance in every aspect of our life? From the way we interact with others, to the sharpness of our minds, to the ability to perform at the gym, to our endurance with our performance on every level, both physically and mentally. What if we were able to push the boundaries in everything we do on a consistent basis, owing to one single ingredient? Wouldn't you then view the word discipline from a positive standpoint?

Thus, if we can master the positive emotions attached to the word discipline and phase out the negative connotations we attach to it, we are far more likely to WANT to have discipline in our lives. It will become part of our DNA, and in time we won't even think about it. Much like how we brush our teeth every night and every morning. It's not something we think about, we just do it. It's part of our routine. Well, actually, it's discipline. You have disciplined yourself to do such an action as you understand the results of doing so and equally the results if you didn't carry it out. Why is it different, then, to have discipline, when it comes to time management (blocking of time), focus (no distractions), and many other areas that affect our performance?

Being prepared for the unexpected is something that discipline teaches us. But how does discipline become part of our life? We have to work at it every single day and when times get tough, it is easy to give up, it is easy to turn our backs and say, "Well, there's always next time." Well what if there's not a next time? What if it's now or never, as I found out firsthand and write about in Chapter 2 of this book.

The hunters in this life, aka the ones who take action and carry out what they say they are going to do, have discipline to help them achieve this, and are not afraid of either the positive or the negative connotations associated with the word. It is just an act, a sense of being, something ingrained in their DNA. Personally, I have instilled discipline in every single corner of my life. From my sleeping habits, to my water intake, nutrition, exercise, and sunlight needs, to time blocking for work, to spending time with my family. I define what "spending time with my family" actually means, though. I like to get more granular with how I spend my time, so it has meaning and purpose. This is a big part of discipline, because when descriptions are vague, we are less likely to do it. For example, if I write on my calendar "spend time with family" and block out the time, I may spend the time feeling concerned about emails I should reply to, or work I should be carrying out. However, if I write in my calendar, "Family time: build a train set, work on the dinosaur puzzle, race toy cars, go to the park," I am far more likely to be focused on the task at hand that I have scheduled in my calendar, and carry out these actions, versus just writing, "spend time with my children." Because what will happen? What do most do when saying they are spending time with their family? They will still pick up their phones, check their email, reply to a comment on social media, send out a text message, which defeats the purpose of setting aside family time. Now the activities each day may vary, especially if you have young children, and that's ok, but if you aren't intentional about how you are going to spend that time, then it is less likely to happen.

You could list one task each day that you would like to accomplish. Just one. You could start with committing to drinking one gallon of water a day. You could start with making your bed each morning or ensuring you sleep eight hours a night. All of those tasks require minimal effort, and yet have a profound effect on the chemistry in your brain. You are training your brain to view those tasks as productive and giving yourself a feeling of accomplishment as well as showing your brain that you can do the simple tasks that over time become good habits. You have to start with the simple tasks first, master those, and then progress to more challenging tasks, such as nutrition or exercise, or time blocking an end to your day versus just a start to your day. Monitor this for 60 days and notice the difference at the end. You won't want to go backwards, you will want to continue in your efforts to create other areas of your life to have discipline.

I also want to address the fact that many will tell you that sometimes you should just "switch off." What does that actually mean, though? What it means to one person could mean something entirely different to another. As an example, my switching off is switching off my thoughts to my tasks that lay ahead by focusing on training with my fellow athletes every single morning, consistently. I am not concerned or excited about what the day will bring at that moment. I am just concentrating on what I'm experiencing in the training center—the sweat, the focus, and the determination to finish what I had set out to accomplish in those 60 minutes with my fellow athletes. On the other hand, switching off, to me, also means drowning out noise from electronics and surrounding myself in nature. But even then, I am intentional about my time so I am not technically switching off, but merely switching my focus. If we learn to use those words "switching focus" versus "switching off" we are far more likely to remain disciplined and intent in our actions.

Many believe that grit is either something you have or you don't and cannot be taught. This is not true. As with many things in life, grit can be taught, as long as you have a system and process.

Grit is a Process

Earlier, I wrote about Nick Saban having tremendous discipline for himself, his players, and his coaches. What contributes to that discipline is a process. Grit is a process. Grit is not something that happens overnight. As of the publication of this book, Nick Saban has won nine SEC West titles, eight SEC championships, six national championships, and had 22 bowl appearances with the University of Alabama. Success of that magnitude did not happen through discipline alone, nor did it happen over a short time frame. Nick Saban had a process. Michael Jordan, who won six NBA championships with the Chicago Bulls, did so, because he has a process. And he followed that process with discipline.

Another example of something many believe you either have or you don't have is creativity. Actually, that theory is proven wrong by many researchers, psychologists, and educators, with Mihaly Csikszentmihalyi being one of them. He wrote, "Creativity results from the interaction of a system composed of three elements: a culture that contains symbolic rules, a person who brings novelty into the symbolic domain, and a field of experts who recognize and validate the innovation".[6] In other words, creativity is not just an individual trait, but a social and environmental system in which it is recognized and valued. So too can be said of grit. When we think of grit as a process that can be taught, via a system, it opens up a realm of opportunity for us to be more open to tap into the tools to develop that grit. The introduction of grit as a system is discussed later in this book, in Chapter 5. The environment we create around us influences how far we are willing to tap into our grit and practice the skill sets needed to master it for when grit chooses us. If we choose our grit before it chooses us, our ability to get through tough situations will become easier over time. We will also be far more likely to develop Innovative solutions to reframe how we view the grit, to change it from a negative to a positive, ultimately impacting not just ourselves, but those around us.

Grit Creates Hope in Others

Another incredible athlete and boxing legend who I had the privilege of interviewing is the legendary athlete "Irish" Micky Ward, American former professional boxer and light welterweight champion. His story became well known through the 2012 movie *The Fighter* in which Mark Wahlberg played Micky Ward, and Christian Bale played his brother, Dicky Ecklund. During our interview, Micky said something so profound that it became the basis of this section. He said, "Grit creates hope in others and it helps others believe they can have grit. They just have to go to that place—don't be scared." It is so true that grit does provide hope in others that they can achieve greatness too. Micky didn't have a specific goal when he started to box. He said he wanted to see how far he could go in boxing and if he could make a living out of it, but he didn't have a specific end goal in mind. He just kept going and going. What Micky did was focus on the process, not the outcome. Even deeper than that, he concentrated on the smaller tasks he needed to do to achieve his goals. For Micky, this meant surrounding himself with the right people. He admits in his twenties he got rid of a lot of people around him who didn't believe in him or serve him in the way he needed. He started to create and build his own "culture of excellence," which you will learn more about in Chapters 2 and 3 of this book.

Even when others doubted Micky and thought he wouldn't make it, he didn't give up and he held onto his own belief, his own hope. When others didn't believe in him, it just fueled the fire even more. He claimed it was "lighter fluid to the fire" and it made him want to blow up in a big way and show others what he could do. Every time he failed, he got back up, learning from his mistakes, learning from others, learning how to get back up and fight harder the next time. He had a belief that he could do more and was better than others viewed him to be. Micky always carried the belief in his heart that he could do it. He always listened to himself and said, "Don't listen to the naysayers." If he had listened to them he would never have achieved what he has today.

But why are so many scared to go to that place of uneasiness? I call it the fear zone. It sits right outside of your comfort zone, but just to the right of that fear zone is your learning zone. This is where the magic happens, because your brain suddenly realizes you can do it, and to the right of the learning zone is where greatness occurs, in the growth zone. One of the reasons many are afraid to go to the fear zone or stay in that fear is because their brains are doing what they think is best—protecting them from the unknown. However, that's why there are so many people unfulfilled and not aligning with their purpose. They are afraid to do so as they don't know the outcome. Instead of focusing on the outcome, focus on the process, just like Bruce Gradowski and Micky Ward did. How will we ever change our habits to carry out the tasks needed if we don't provide our brain with the information it needs to be able to make those changes, also known as neuroplasticity? Instead of allowing our thoughts to control us, we need to be in control of our thoughts. Every single day. We have to do uncomfortable things, things that scare us, things that make us want to run straight back to our comfort zone.

Micky did exactly that by explaining that when he thought something through and wasn't sure if he could get through it, he made the choice to give it everything he had, and then suddenly realized that he could do it. He got out of his comfort zone, into the fear zone. That led him into the learning zone, which got him into the growth zone, and that's how he achieved what he has, being the light welterweight champion with 38 wins, 27 of them knockout wins, with three of the best fights in history with Arturo Galli. One of Micky's tricks he uses to stay in the fear zone is that he knows the pain won't last forever. It's only a few more minutes in that round. When I asked him what he'd say to someone who says, "I'll just do it tomorrow," his response was "Tomorrow never comes." That's a favorite saying of mine as well. Micky went on to say, "Once you put your mind into the state of 'I can't do it,' it's very difficult to get your mind back in the game of 'I can do it.' So don't stop. Stay on it. Take a break later."

The Grit You Choose and the Grit You Don't

Look back at situations in your life that proved to be tough for you. It could have been the death of a sibling, a parent, a child, or a divorce. Maybe it was a mother, father, or a caregiver leaving you, bullying in elementary school, problems in high school, an alcoholic parent, the loss of a job. All of these things and more require an element of grit to get through. If you believe you don't have grit, I challenge you to look back at these situations in life and review how you dealt with it.

No matter how fast or slow, you have used grit at some point in your life. As a baby, we all had grit. We learned how to crawl, we learned how to walk, we learned how to talk. All of this required various elements of grit. How many times did you fall over as a baby, a toddler, a young child? So many times you don't remember. But you got back up each and every *time*. So true is the same philosophy in adulthood. You get knocked down, you get back up, but you get up stronger. Why? Because you followed a system without even knowing it. You followed the Global G.R.I.T. System™ (discussed in detail in Chapter 5 of this book) without realizing it. Bruce suggests that if you feel you haven't used grit before, start slow, start somewhere. The nights when you put your children to bed and they aren't behaving in the way you would like them to, use grit in that moment. Respond differently. In other words, one can reframe how they think about a situation, no matter how tough. The techniques of reframing how we think are discussed, at length, in Chapter 7 of this book.

Additionally, at some point in your life you have displayed grit whether you know it or not, but as Bruce points out, you also choose whether you stop using it and give in. It's in that very moment when you need to dig deeper and tap into extra grit so when you look back you can say "I gave it my all." You live and learn from what you do. Your brain is constantly changing and shaping how you view the environment around you.[7] So use that to your advantage.

If you become proficient in every element of the Global G.R.I.T. System™ (which is introduced in Chapter 4 of this book), what you can achieve will be immense and help you identify solutions to problems you may be facing as a seasoned leader, an aspiring leader, or a new leader, or quite simply in life, generally. Just remember, as Micky says, "Hard times don't last forever, but you are the one that has to look in the mirror and ask yourself, 'Did I give it my all or not?' Only you will know." That's the big difference between those who use their grit versus the ones that don't. Choose your grit before it chooses you. Because it will choose you if it hasn't already. How you respond will affect your brain patterns and either strengthen your response in a positive or negative way.[8] Hunters choose their grit, every single day, until it becomes part of their DNA. Then it isn't a choice anymore, it becomes a habit. It becomes a part of them. So, what can you do today to shape your tomorrow? Answer: Choose your grit. And if you still don't want to choose your grit, well, enjoy the hunt. The long grass is calming.

Choose your Grit.

Trust the Process.

Adopt the System.

"Don't be afraid to step into the light, for It illuminates the path that reveals your authentic solf and banishes the darkness of the past."

Lara Jones

10 Key Leadership Lessons From This Chapter:

- Choose your grit before it chooses you.

- Grit is a process and can be taught and thus developed in anyone.

- We all have grit, we just have to use the tools in the Global G.R.I.T. System™ to awaken them.

- Use the term "switching focus" versus "switching off." Switching off means different things to different people.

- Be intentional and specific with your time, including your down time.

- When times get tough, that's when the real learning happens.

- Grit impacts others to believe they can do it too.

- Do it now, tomorrow never comes.

- Start with one thing to instill discipline until it becomes a habit, then move onto another.

- The lion is always watching. So if you see long wavering grass nearby, either join them, or run.

CHAPTER 2

The Birth of Grit

"It ain't how hard you hit. It's about how hard you get hit and keep moving forward."

Rocky Balboa

The Grit That I Chose

May 25, 2016. The date that changed my life. It was on this day that I packed a suitcase, my laptop, and just me and my brain stepped on a plane, heading for the United States of America. I didn't want to become an expert in grit but I am about to tell you why I did.

I grew up in England, the United Kingdom. I was a happy child, always with a big smile on my face, showing all my teeth when smiling, which has become a signature of mine, and always had a zest for life. I was often being told off at primary school for laughing or giggling too much and was sent outside of the classroom on some occasions or separated from friends owing to too much fun. I always had time for others and made friends easily.

As I grew up, though, I faced challenges that involved deep trauma, including experiencing a traumatic event in my teenage years of sexual assault that was a heinous violation of my boundaries and had a profound impact on my trust for others and haunted me for years until I felt ready to talk about it at the age of 21. I often found myself dealing with situations, alone, and figuring out what was next. But often it was through decisions I had made or situations I found myself in, owing to the decisions I had made, that led me having to get through some incredibly tough times. When I was 28 I lost my Omi, aka my grandmother (she was German), and my marriage the same year. My Omi and my United States Air Force (USAF) husband were the only two people in the world I felt the closest to in my life at that time because of decisions I had made earlier in my life which led to isolation from my family for several years. I watched my Omi pass away and was by her bedside in the hospital, and shortly after I discovered my husband had betrayed me in multiple ways, which devastated and broke me to my core. I found myself divorced at the age of 29 from someone I had given up my family for. A difficult decision, but I knew the trust could never be present in the same way it had been before and knew there would be more torment if I stayed than if I left. I chose the grit of starting over to pursue a new path of courage and strength rather than choosing the grit of staying and potentially being stuck in a cycle of pain and mistrust. That same year I had left an incredible position in a company, as I was supposed to be moving to the U.S. a few months later with my then husband. I found myself, once again, isolated and alone.

One of those other tough times, at the age of 30, included being severely beaten, causing trauma to my chest, neck, and face, with my face turning black and blue. That person was eventually convicted, but it took two years, moving to the other side of the country, police protection, a restraining order, and dealing with death threats every single day, along with harrowing nightmares. That person was convicted by a jury in April of 2016.

It was at that moment that I realized in order to find that happy young child again, I needed to make serious changes. I needed to choose my grit before grit kept choosing me. I had a very comfortable life in England and had earned well during my career over there, with helping a vending company in a very saturated market grow from approximately 5 million to around 50 million dollars over a few years. I loved my time with that company, making some lifelong friends, and learning incredible skills and valuable lessons. I had actually left that company two months before my grandma passed away and my husband betrayed me. I was offered my position back in the company after they discovered that I was not leaving for the U.S. at that time, due to my divorce, but I have never been a believer in going backward, only forward. I worked freelance for a while as a sales and marketing director, coaching and training sales teams, enhancing performance in leaders, and building companies from the ground up. I focused on new business sales for organizations, which meant building relationships from scratch, cold calling, all the practices that many did not want to endure. I trained them and built companies. I left a very comfortable life, financially, in England, the day I decided to make the move. Why did I do it? Because I was unhappy with my environment. I didn't have my "culture of excellence" around me that I strived for. I didn't like the mindset of those around me at the time. I knew I wanted more in my life and needed to show others that they don't have to live a life of misery, working until age 65 then retiring and dying. I had that hunter mentality in me, and felt it was my duty to share it with the world. So right before my thirty-second birthday I got on a plane to the United States of America and never returned.

Ripping the Comfort Blanket Away

The grit I chose in making that decision to get on a plane meant ripping the comfort blanket away, taking away any security and putting myself through many ups and downs, including not being able to eat for three days because I only had money to pay for a roof over my head, not lodging and food. I chose to have a roof over my head. I only gave myself a plan A. There was no plan B. In order to stay committed on the path, you commit to one plan. Plan A.

I met many people along my journey and learned about the lives of others and what drove them to do what they do in life. They found my courage fascinating, daunting, and risky to give up a life I had known and start again at the age of 32. A few of the people I met along the way were incredibly kind to me, lending a car at one point, with another friend offering a room in her house for me to stay in for as long as I needed. I made those friends on my journey to prove to others what is possible once you rip the comfort blanket away and don't have any choice BUT to either succeed or fail. And if you fail, you get back up. You learn from it, you try again, you use everything you have learned and build something better next time.

Eighteen months after being in the United States, I met my now husband. A United States Marine Corps Veteran who served long before I met him. And when we did meet, he did not have any money, much like myself. I recognized that he too had dreams but didn't know how to act on them. I had the ability to act on anything someone gave me but didn't always know the dreams or path I was on, I just knew I needed to impact others. Thus, a perfect match. After we met, the grit I chose included having to say my goodbyes to my grandfather, aka Opi, over Facetime, right before he passed away as I couldn't leave the country at that point because I was going through the process of applying for my Green Card and adjusting my status. I started my company, Be a Legend, in the United States of America as it was my only source of income to be able to survive. But I didn't start it to just "survive." I started it for many reasons. For others to believe they can do something, they first have to see it. Look at Roger Bannister and the four-minute mile. Many thought it was unachievable and not possible for a human being to run a four-minute mile, but Roger Bannister proved them wrong. All of a sudden, not long after, others were able to achieve it. I wanted to do the same thing—to prove to others that you can have nothing and build a life you want from nothing, with nothing, as long as you have the determination to do so and reframe how you look at situations to be a positive rather than a negative.

A year after my husband and I got married, we welcomed our first son while I was building the business. A short while later, we welcomed our second son into the world, while I was expanding the business. Just a few months after that, we were thrilled to learn of our third son that surprised us and meant all three of our children would be incredibly close in age, growing up as the three musketeers. I finally felt that the grit I had chosen had gotten me to this point in my life where I was extremely happy, living the life I had always wanted, regardless of the struggles along the way. It was all part of my growth and getting out of my comfort zone, into my fear zone, to achieve my learning zone to show others and myself what could be done and that it CAN be done, in order to achieve the growth zone. I finally felt that I had escaped my trauma, transformed it into something that gave me a beautiful life instead.

But I was wrong. Very wrong. In one day, one moment, everything changed. The day I thought would never come because of the life I had carved for myself. But this is proof that no matter how hard we try, we can not escape adversity. It will come for all of us in one form or another. How prepared you are for that grit that chooses you will define and shape who you are.

The Grit That Chose Me

September 2, 2021. I recall the screaming, seeing blood-soaked clothes, blood-soaked mats, blood-soaked towels, a blood-soaked floor. And me. Holding my dead son's body in my hands. Lifeless. No signs of life whatsoever. Wishing, hoping, pleading, that this was one huge nightmare and that my son would show signs of life.

I was at home at the time and had experienced pain. I was pregnant, in my second trimester with our third son, who just days earlier was perfectly healthy with a strong heartbeat. I had experienced pain and phoned the on-call doctor who didn't believe there was anything to worry about and to come in the next day to be checked. That next day never came.

I had put my living children to bed, who were one and two and a half at the time. I sang to them, read to them, and tucked them in for the night. I kissed their heads goodnight, and shut their door and said "see you in the morning." That morning didn't come for their brother, and it very nearly didn't come for me.

About 45 minutes after having that phone call with the doctor, and after putting my living children to bed, I was laying down when all of a sudden I heard a "pop"—the sound of my water breaking, a sound that echoes in my head to this day. All of a sudden there was amniotic fluid everywhere. All over the sheets, all over the floor, and I knew I was in labor and my son was coming, and coming quickly. There was no time to get to the hospital, this was my third child. He came quickly, and I knew I was going to have to deliver my child, myself. I yelled out to my husband and told him to call emergency services. He stared at me in horror, not realizing what was taking place, as he was in disbelief. The look on his face is one that will haunt me forever. I had to take action, this was not a time for me to wonder why. Why me? Why now? Why like this? I just had to deliver my son and deal with the aftermath later. I wasn't expecting what was to come next. I didn't really know what to expect.

I delivered his lifeless body and still remember his legs so limp, his head dropping and no signs of life whatsoever, and I just started sobbing, and screaming "No, no, no." I knew he had died and there was nothing I could do to get him to come back to life. He looked so perfect, albeit small. We had already named him just days prior, "Jack Josef Jones," with a sweet nickname of "little JJ." I just sobbed and in that moment I wanted to die alongside him. I wanted my son back. I wanted to hear him cry. I wanted to hear his breathing. I wanted to see him open his eyes. I wanted his fingers to grab mine and clasp around them like many newborn babies do.

Emergency services arrived but they were seven minutes too late to help with the delivery and arrived after I had delivered him. They helped finish the process of delivering him by cutting his umbilical cord. They laid him down on the floor, covering him with a blanket. The image of his little hand sticking out from under the sheet is still with me to this very day. This should never have happened, but it did. There was no reason, no warning, nothing that prepared me for holding my son's lifeless body and screaming out to the world my pain and hurt that was so deep, I felt like I couldn't breathe and that I would die too. That feeling wasn't just a feeling, but it was what I was actually experiencing as one by one my organs started to shut down from the sheer amount of blood loss that had occurred. I was completely oblivious to this fact, but recall seeing the blood-soaked clothes, the blood-soaked mat I was lying on that used to be white. And I remember the male paramedic saying, "We need to get you to hospital, you are hemorrhaging." I recall the female paramedic, who was standing over me as I sobbed, saying, "Why did he die, what did I do?" and she kept saying, "It's not your fault, it's not your fault." The reality is something had gone wrong, but to this day I will never know what.

My torment wasn't over. The ambulance rushed me to hospital, the sight of the flashing lights outside of my home are still vivid to this day, and I remember lying in the ambulance, with my dead son, and I was struggling to catch my breath through my sobbing and screaming. I arrived at the ER and they immediately hooked me up to an IV and monitored my blood pressure along with telling me I had a retained placenta. This should have been removed within thirty minutes of giving birth, but for whatever reason, still unknown to this day, the on-call doctor had canceled my blood transfusion and didn't get me into surgery immediately, claiming she could stabilize me without the need for any of that. She was wrong. Dangerously wrong.

About three to four hours went by and suddenly I sat bolt upright and I knew something terrible was about to unfold. I knew I was dying. I looked my husband in his eyes and said, "Get me water, I'm going to die." He said, "No, you are going to have surgery at some point, you can't have water." He didn't realize the gravity of the situation at that point as the machines had not picked up what I was feeling. It felt like every inch of water was draining from my body, and I had an intense thirst that was so bad I wanted pints and pints of water. So I shouted back, "Get me water, I'm going to die!" As stubborn as he was, he likes to be right, and he once again refused, saying that it was dangerous if I drank water before surgery. All of a sudden my eyesight started to tunnel, my hearing started to muffle, my speech started to slur, my coordination started to go, and I missed hitting the button for the nurse. I knew at that moment I had to take responsibility and take matters into my own hands otherwise my husband, who had seen his son die, would have also witnessed his wife die. I shouted out "Nurse" as best as I could, and as a nurse came into the room, she shone a flashlight into my eyes. At that point my pupils stopped responding because of the lack of oxygen and lack of blood flow to my eyes. All of a sudden the blood pressure machine began to beep as my blood pressure started to plummet. The nurse yelled out, "Emergency blood transfusion, emergency blood transfusion," and before I knew it there were half a dozen doctors and nurses around my bedside. They had brought a crash cart into my room and my blood pressure continued to plummet and I knew I was about to die. I said my goodbyes to my husband and made him vow to always put the children first and look after them, and I stared at the doctor and asked, "Am I going to die?" hoping her response would be a firm "No," but she simply stared at me and said, "Not on my watch" as they frantically tried to save my life. And then I thought, "Well Jack needs me too." But if I died with him, what would happen to my living children? My husband would be widowed, my children left with no mother. The last time my children saw me, they heard me say "See you in the morning," and then I closed their door. I was determined to see them in the morning.

As my blood pressure continued to plummet, it got down as low as 53/37. I knew in that moment by the next beep and flash of the machine I would be dead. I had to decide how I was going to take control of the situation. There was nothing I could do from a physical standpoint, and I had to hope that the doctors and nurses would save me. I could hear the nurses to my left arguing because they couldn't get the 16 gauge needle into my collapsed veins. I had lost so much blood that one by one my organs were shutting down, and my heart wasn't able to pump enough blood around my body to reach all of my organs. I had two choices. One, accept it and die or two, accept it and control the only part of myself that I could control. My mind. I chose two. I knew I couldn't panic, I would die quicker if I did. I had to somehow slow my heart rate down to give the nurses more time to figure out how to get the needle in me with the emergency blood transfusion my body needed. And in those last few moments before I was about to flatline, I told myself I will be resuscitated and I *will* come back because I have to. I am too young to die and have so much more to offer others. I have living children at home that need their mother, and I wasn't about to let my husband remarry and have someone else bring up my children. I then proceeded to close my eyes and I imagined myself back at home with my living children. I carried out the five, four, three, two, one technique that I have taught many others and said what are five things I can see, four things I can hear, three things I can feel, two things I can smell, and one thing I can taste. It helps reduce anxiety and tricks the brain into feeling something other than what is actually going on. In doing so, my brain really believed I was with my children. I can still picture that scene today of what I imagined and can hear my living children laughing, giggling, and playing. In doing what I did, I slowed my heart rate down and my blood pressure suddenly stopped falling and held at 53/37 long enough for the nurses to figure out how to get the needle in me with the blood that saved my life. It felt like I was in a crumpled heap on the floor and suddenly I was being picked up by my head as I felt the blood pour back into me. I was then rushed into surgery to remove the placenta and stop the internal bleeding.

When I awoke from surgery I was in the ER. I had already delivered my son at home, so I was not in the maternity ward. The nurses were perhaps not used to my situation and thus reacted in a rather matter of fact way. The first question I was asked after I awoke from surgery was, "Do you want to have your son buried or cremated?" Followed by, "What funeral directors do you want to use? We have to know where to transport his body. We need to know within 24 hours. Here's the paperwork you need to fill out." It was all so much to take in. After another few hours, and after making sure I was stable, I was allowed to go home. In a wheelchair, with no baby. With only my husband for support. And told to follow up with my doctor the next day. The next day came. I phoned but received no phone call from the doctor. The following day came, no phone call from the doctor. A week later, I finally received a call from the doctor only to be told they couldn't get me in to see me for another 30 days. Thirty days! It may as well have been a lifetime. The darkness I felt during that time period was intense and I felt as though all of the walls were closing in on me. I couldn't walk unassisted and couldn't drive. I had anemia as a result of the blood loss and I was told that the hospital staff hadn't given me quite enough blood. When that 30 days did come, the doctor spent all of 60 seconds with me saying he had to rush off to deliver a baby and that I will be okay and to just have another baby. Needless to say, he was not part of my "culture of excellence" I had strived to find after I left the country I grew up in.

When I came home from the hospital, at around 8:00 am the following day, following the tragedy of my son's passing and nearly my own, my children had just started to wake up for the day. They had no idea of the awful tragedy that had just occurred some 12 hours earlier and how close they were to never seeing their mother again. I had to explain to my eldest what had happened, as he asked about Jack. With tears streaming down my face, I had to tell him the heartbreaking news that he would never get to grow up with his brother, he wouldn't get to play with him, and he wouldn't get to hug him. It was so incredibly tragic, as he just stared at me solemnly, not quite comprehending everything I was saying.

A few days later, my husband and I got to spend time alone with our son, Jack, at the funeral home. It was not long enough. No amount of hours would have felt long enough. I had seen a dead adult before (my British grandmother), but never a baby. When I held my baby after delivering him, even though he had died at that point, he just looked like he was sleeping and was warm. Now, my son was ice cold and wrapped in a blanket, looking peaceful, but it devastated me to see my child in a crib, not opening his eyes, not crying out to be cradled, not being able to feed him. I picked him up immediately and started to rock him. I told him how much I loved him, and that I was sorry I couldn't bring him back to life and sorry for whatever had killed him. To this day, I still don't have the answers. The autopsy revealed he was a perfectly healthy little boy. My tests also came back perfectly healthy, and nobody knows what happened. I was told that I had to accept that I will never know, which is incredibly difficult for someone of my personality who always likes to look at solutions rather than problems, and believes there is a "fix" for every problem. Until that day. Until I realized I can't "fix" my dead child, or all of the other babies, children, and others who have died. After singing to my Jack, reading a story to him, kissing him on his head, putting his little hand in mine, and cradling him, I finally laid him to rest, back in his crib, where the hardest thing I have ever had to do was about to unfold. Giving birth to him and holding his lifeless body until emergency services arrived was not the hardest part of this process, saying goodbye to my husband as I lay dying in the hospital bed as one by one my organs were shutting down was not the hardest part of this process, seeing my blood pressure drop to 53/37, knowing that the next time it flashed I wouldn't know because I would have flatlined, was not the hardest part. No, the hardest part of this entire process was having to say goodbye to my son and leave him in that crib while I had to walk out of this huge room, where the crib looked so tiny, and close the door without saying the words "see you in the morning" like I did to my living children, every night. I wasn't going to see him in the morning, like my living children, and I wasn't able to just open the door back up. I knew this was the last time I would ever see my son's body.

I chose to have Jack cremated as I couldn't bear the thought of his being buried in a cemetery, alone, without his mommy and daddy visiting him every single day, which would have proved incredibly difficult with our living children. I also wanted to bring him home. I wanted his brothers to be able to "meet" him. So a few days after I said my goodbyes, our Jack was cremated. We brought him home, in his urn. Not the welcome home I had ever dreamed of when I was carrying him through the front door, but at least I got to bring him home, even if it meant in an urn. His room we had created for him sat there empty. Waiting for him to come home. A bassinet that would never be used by him. A closet filled with baby clothes that had to be emptied. A crib mobile that will never have his eyes watching it back and forth as it twirls around with the sun shining on it. His room just remained there, empty.

The very next day, after I had come back home from hospital and two days since Jack passed away and I nearly died, all of a sudden, my husband yelled out to me to come quickly outside. And at that moment, about 15 or so beautiful butterflies flew off the side of our house. We had never seen a butterfly at our property until that day. I knew it was a sign from my Jack. For months afterwards I continued to see butterflies but more prominently. A beautiful yellow monarch butterfly would fly by at the times I felt the most sad, as if he knew and would come and say hello.

I ended up sleeping on the couch for four months as I couldn't bring myself to be upstairs where the tragedy had taken place and it would have taken about 10 minutes to walk up the stairs, because of my anemia. It wasn't until January of 2022 that something in me switched and realized that every day that had gone by since my tragic loss, I had actually been very slowly trying to walk through thick mud in deep trenches that felt like I was going nowhere, but hour by hour, half a day by half a day, I made progress. I was able to look back at the process I had just been through for the past four months and realized that I had made it through some of the toughest days. The day came where I celebrated putting a little makeup on for the first time in four months. I was able to get dressed for the whole day, instead of for an hour or two. I was able to shower again in my own bathroom rather than my living children's bathroom. These were all incredible wins for me that I didn't realize had happened until I stopped, paused and reflected on my progress within those four months.

I had attempted to attend a support group about six weeks after I lost my Jack, but I didn't like it, so many were so much further ahead in the process than I, and I knew I needed to be around others who were in a similar situation to me who wanted to find a source of healing for the raw pain that occurred every single day. I eventually found that source, in the name of "Heaven Hummingbirds" that my friend and fellow athlete, Jennifer Butson, founded under the support of Dignity Health, whose parent company is CommonSpirit Health. It is an incredible support group for parents who have lost children through pregnancy or during infancy. I remember attending my very first Heaven Hummingbirds support group, and only two of us were in attendance who had lost children. But I remember hearing the other mother's story and feeling such pain, not just from my loss but also from hers. I suddenly realized I was now in a club I didn't want to be in. I was part of a group of people I didn't want to be part of, but I couldn't change it, and realized that I needed to start rethinking how I was looking at my situation.

So I continued to attend, month after month. What many didn't realize is that I am the CEO of the company I was running. I couldn't take time off dedicated solely for grieving. I had a meeting scheduled three days after the loss of my son, and I had other meetings scheduled that very week, but I was able to push those meetings back by two weeks (but the meeting three days after, was a phone call that could not be pushed back). I was not even able to drive when I attended those other meetings, just two weeks later. I had to ask my husband to attend those meetings with me. As he helped in the business at the time, it was a little easier to explain why he was there. What I wasn't prepared for were the pregnancy stories I would subsequently hear or new births of babies. It seemed like everyone was having babies or getting pregnant. I couldn't show emotion or explain what happened to me for fear of them thinking I wasn't competent to be running a business. I also didn't want to put a damper on the incredibly happy news of others. So I pulled from my grit that I had chosen in my life and had learned prior and was able to get the meetings done I needed to get done, and I reframed how I thought in every single one of them. I talk further about reframing thoughts and how I did that in Chapter 7 of this book.

It's Not About Me, It's About Others

When I lay dying on that hospital bed, I vowed that if I survived and got another chance at life, I had one mission and one mission only: to impact at least one person, for at least one day, for every day that I am breathing.

I realized very quickly it wasn't about me, my trauma, what I had been through. It's about others, what they needed, not what I needed. In doing so, it shifted my perspective and I started to see clearly who the right people were to have in my corner and who the wrong people were. I built stronger relationships as a result, building an incredible amount of trust and creating my own "culture of excellence." When I shifted away from my needs and focused on the needs of others, I saw how valued and appreciated people felt and the positive impact I had on their life, which in turn created positivity in my own life. Suddenly the day came when I smiled again, because I realized what my purpose was in my life and I suddenly started to feel fulfilled. I realized that I can impact so many with my story, but not making it about me, making it about them and showing how my grit through severe adversity created new techniques and tools that quite literally saved my life. I knew I had to share this with others. I felt it was my duty. I was creating meaningful change and connection that far surpassed my own individual needs and instead centered around the needs and lives of those around me. I was able to shut off what I needed in those moments and make it all about others. This helped me focus on the task at hand, rather than thinking about what I was going to do for the rest of my life without my son. But this did not come without challenges, and the road ahead was still long. Instead of taking it day by day, which some had suggested, I actually took it hour by hour. Then progressed to half a day by half a day. What was the point in trying to plan weeks ahead, when tomorrow I might not wake up? Yes, those were real feelings I experienced.

Emotional Aftermath and Residual Trauma

I had started to see a trauma counselor and six months later, the diagnosis came: PTSD (Post Traumatic Stress Disorder). I already knew it. I had severe hypervigilance, flashbacks, memory issues, sleep disorder, pain in my joints, anxiety, nightmares, intrusive thoughts that something terrible was going to happen every moment of every day, and intense distress at reminders of the trauma. The list was endless. It felt like my life was going from bad to worse and yet I still had to function for my family, my living children, my team members, my business, my clients. Everything fell on my shoulders as the leader and yet here I was feeling like I was the one who was crumbling every single day but somehow I had to keep it together for everyone else. And now I was dealing with PTSD. What next? I knew I didn't want medication. I wanted to be able to know that when I thought clearly, it was because of my healing and efforts managing my PTSD versus a drug that was inducing it. There are approximately eight million people in the U.S. alone who are diagnosed with PTSD. One in 11 people will be diagnosed with PTSD at some point in their lifetime.[1] This means that the probability of you knowing someone, if not yourself, who has been diagnosed with PTSD is extremely high.

Every Day is a Chance To Be Better

What I learned after this harrowing experience, not just as a leader, but in life, is that I was given a second chance to live that day. I was given a second chance to feel the sun on my skin, to breathe the oxygen we need, to see the nature around us, to feel the water on my feet when I step into the ocean, to hear the rain falling outside, to hear the thunder and see the lightning, to see the lush green in the summer and the crisp brown leaves in the fall and winter. I have the privilege of hearing the chitter chatter and seeing the hustle and bustle in the morning at coffee shops. I can hear the birds singing, my living children's laughter, their crying and screaming. I was given a second chance to hear their footsteps as they run around the house. I was grateful for all of it. I realized it was my time to show what I can do with all that I was grateful for, and to live my second chance with meaning, gratitude, and a focus on impacting others.

I decided to continue to choose my grit, even though I had been through some of life's worst experiences. I knew that in order to impact at least one person, for at least one day, for every day that I am breathing, it had to start with my actions first. So, I joined an incredible training center just 11 months after losing my son and nearly my life. Called Suffer City, it was co-founded by Jason France—athlete and Special Operations Marine Raider. I heard about it from Jennifer Butson, the very lady who founded the Heaven Hummingbirds support group that I attended after my son passed away, and started my journey to become an athlete. I found a community of strong-willed, tough, gritty athletes who gave all they had, even when they didn't feel like they had enough to give. I set a goal when I first walked into that world that I would be among the elite athletes within one year at Suffer City and train with them in their S.O.S. class on a Saturday. Less than a year later, 341 days to be exact, I did it. That test, for females, included running for 25 calories on a "runner," followed by 25 box jumps at a height of 20 inches, 20 thrusters using 25 pound dumbbells, 15 hang cleans at a weight of 85 pounds, 10 deadlifts with a weight of 135 pounds, followed by five pull-ups, a sled push-pull with four 45 pound plates on a sled for approximately 30 meters, finishing off with 25 calories on the airbike. All in under 10 minutes. The first time I took the test to get into the class, I failed. I continued training and never gave up. I surrounded myself with my culture of excellence and took action to achieve my goal of training with the elites. I trained harder, added extra sessions, dialed in my nutrition even more, hired a personal coach at Suffer City, Marcus Neal, who helped me twice a week with my technique. I stayed behind every single day to work on my pull-ups. I did what 99 percent of people aren't willing to do–grit through it (discussed in Chapter 4 of this book). I always said I was the baby cub when I joined these incredible athletes and one day I would be coming for them. During that year I became a fierce lioness and on July 15, 2023 I joined the elites, and my comfort zone, fear zone, learning zone, and growth zone started all over again. And I found myself the baby cub once more. The circle of life. Now the journey starts all over again, only this time, it's with the elites.

The main takeaway from losing my son and nearly my life is this: If you fall, you get back up. And you NEVER give up. That's what leaders do. They face fear, they look into the light, they never give up, and they practice their new skills from what they learned during failure. Over and over and over.

"Through action, a man becomes a hero
Through death, a hero becomes a legend
Through time, a legend becomes a myth
And by learning from the myth
a man takes action"

Unknown

So take action. Now. We come from a place we didn't choose, but we can choose where we are going. No matter if you grew up rich or poor, in happy or unhappy circumstances, we do have a choice where we go from there. There is no cavalry coming to save you, you have to rely on yourself first. Nobody is going to believe in you if you don't believe in yourself first.

We all have the capability to be who we want to be. We just need the tools to learn how to unlock it. You will learn how to unlock these tools in Chapters 6 through 9 of this book.

So ask yourself: What are you doing today to get you to where you need to be tomorrow?

"Do the best you can until you know better.
Then when you know better, do better."

Maya Angelou

10 Key Leadership Lessons From This Chapter:

- Choose your grit before it chooses you, and discover when your grit birthday is.

- If you don't like something, change it. Only you are in control of that.

- Ensure you have the right people in the right seats, on the right bus, and get the wrong people off the bus.

- Create your culture of excellence for you first, then your team.

- Face fear. It starts with you.

- There are four zones: comfort zone, fear zone, learning zone, and growth zone. Don't run back to your comfort zone when times get tough in your fear zone, Learn new techniques and strategies to get you through to your learning zone to achieve your growth zone. Lead a team through the fear and show them how to achieve growth.

- Always be prepared for adversity. Be prepared as a leader, be prepared for your team.

- It's not about you, it's about others. Impact your team in meaningful ways, and see how your own life is impacted.

- Even when you think you are over the worst when the storm hits, there's always the aftermath that has to be dealt with and if ignored, could be detrimental to your team.

- If you fall or any member of your team falls, get back up. Help them get back up, and NEVER give up.

- Always ask yourself: "What are you doing today to get you to where you need to be, tomorrow?"

burned much of its fuel and you believe that the fire will burn out, what you fail to realize is that there is still usable energy within that piece of fuel. You just have to learn how to use it in a way that will ignite a much bigger fire than before. But where do we start?

Grit is associated with passion and perseverance for long-term goals.[2] Although these traits of passion and perseverance are necessary, why is it that so many give up on their dreams? They have the passion, and in many cases have the perseverance, but still don't reach their goals?

The problem lies in the fact that many start their journey with their passion and have a desire to do well, but if a setback happens, some will give up. If a few more setbacks happen many will give up entirely. When reality hits and they face challenges while continuing to pursue their dream, they may in fact become burnt out or feel that other obligations get in their way, so they give up. In time, their passion dies and their goal becomes a distant memory. Therefore, grit is not just defined as passion and perseverance but the ability to adapt, adjust, and learn from experiences in order to keep going even through failures, multiple setbacks, and adversity. But what if you have never had a life experience that can teach the values of what adapting, adjusting, and learning really looks like?

Myth: Grit can only be developed in those born with that trait.

Wrong. Another myth is the belief that grit is solely in those who are born with it, that it is a fixed trait that cannot be developed. The very fact that one may think that grit cannot be cultivated and taught is not a problem with grit itself in that individual, but rather the mindset of that individual. They are stuck in the fear zone and run back and forth to and from the comfort zone, never exiting the other side of the fear into the learning zone to teach their brains how grit can be developed, which ultimately leads to the growth zone. Belief plays a strong role in how we not only establish grit, but our ability to continue on that path.[3]

Myth: Grit isn't as important as the other elements of leadership.

Wrong. Although there are crucial elements of leadership that are absolutely essential, including communication, emotional intelligence, accountability, and decision making, among many others, the most important element is grit. Why? Because without it, you may as well forget about the rest of them. Others in your team will follow what you do as a leader. You set the example. You show them why it needs to be done and how. If you want others to never give up, you have to show them that you haven't, and never will. It starts with you.

With grit it's not just about working hard, but inspiring, motivating, providing confidence, and building a culture for others to aspire to. A culture of excellence. You decide your team's culture. You decide what is acceptable and what is not acceptable. You decide when to change the path and when to stick with it, but you also decide whether your team members give up or not because they are watching, learning, and listening from you. You have to give it everything you have, know when to alter the course if it's not working, and when to stick with it, because what you are aiming for may very well be right around the corner. When you believe in yourself first and foremost and believe in your team members, grit will be instilled in each and every one of your leaders and each and everyone of your team members. With this grit unbelievable achievements can occur. Visualize it, see it happening, and play that out in your mind every single moment and it will happen. It might not be today, it might not be tomorrow, but one day what you set out to achieve will happen. Every moment counts. Not just when you are awake, but also when you are sleeping, which allows you time to rest and recover so your brain can be sharp, grow, improve, and focus.

When adversity, obstacles, and setbacks occur, having grit is what will get you through those moments and help you see the actions you need to take to continue to persevere. Picking yourself back up and talking to yourself in a powerful, positive way will reinforce the message that you absolutely can and absolutely will, no matter what.

Myth: Relentless grit is a grind and leads to burnout.

Wrong. Both grit and resilience are positively associated with well-being and negatively associated with burnout.[4] In fact, having relentless grit increases resilience and the ability to overcome challenges and just "get it done." Take Thomas Edison as an example. He failed many times before inventing the light bulb and had he not had relentless grit, the light bulb would have emerged much later than it did. He never gave up. It led him to success and he did not experience burnout. Grit doesn't lead to burnout. Not taking care of oneself leads to burnout. However, when grit becomes a grind is when you have perseverance without passion. This is a grind, but this is not grit. The two are often confused.[5]

The myths around the idea that working hard and using grit will lead to burnout is only true if one does not take care of oneself. Think of it like this: your body is your hardware. Much like a computer. Your organs are the software, much like the operating system of a computer. If you don't charge your computer, what happens? The battery runs out. If you continue to drive your computer into the ground and overload it with information, if you don't restart it from time to time to allow a reboot, don't charge it efficiently when it needs to be charged, then what will happen? You will end up trading it within two to three years, maybe four at a stretch. But it's highly unlikely you will reach the five-year mark if you abuse it and don't treat it with care and give it what it needs. Why do you think the human body is any different? Now human bodies can last for many, many years before they start having issues, but the principle is the same. We care so much as a society about the well being of our heart, our lungs, our skin. But what about your brain? Your brain is an organ too. It is a large part of the software. So give it what it needs. For example, how much water have you had today? If it is toward the end of the day for you and you haven't had at least a gallon, you could very well be dehydrated. How much sleep did you get last night? If it wasn't at least seven hours or more, your brain cannot function at its optimum level.[6] What about your nutrition? How many foods do you eat that are processed? Did you know the more processed foods you eat, the higher your inflammation? They alter the bacteria that lives in your gut, which interacts with your immune system, which leads to inflammation.[7] Do you elevate your heart rate each day or a few times a week through exercise?

The basics seem just that: basic. But why do we find them so difficult to do when they really are the basics to an incredibly high functioning body and thus high functioning brain? A lack of these four pillars of health may lead to neuropsychiatric disorders eventually, particularly if one has a predisposition to a neuropsychiatric disorder and creates an environment in which this can form.[8]

My good friend and performance physio, Sarah Powell, who has completed more than 13 years in post doctoral education to specialize in spine and orthopedics with a fellowship in orthopedic manual physical therapy, reminded me of a fifth pillar: the sun. Being out in the sunlight for a few minutes each day helps to boost serotonin in our brain that helps to keep us calm, positive, and focused. It also provides the Vitamin D our brains need for promoting the production of neurotransmitters, supporting nerve growth and development, and reducing inflammation in the brain. Additionally, even though skin cancer is associated with too much ultraviolet radiation (UVR) exposure, too little exposure actually increases the risk of other cancers such as breast, ovarian, colon, pancreatic, prostate, and many others. This is why living at higher latitudes increases the risk of these cancers and why it is recommended for a little sun exposure for a few minutes a day, every day.[9] So grit itself does not lead to burnout. But carrying out any tasks without taking care of yourself through the five pillars will.

Myth: Work engagement doesn't affect my performance with grit.

Wrong. The relationship between grit and creativity in the workplace is directly correlated to how engaged one is in their work environment and if their values align with that of their team and company.[10] In other words, getting the right people in the right seats on the right bus and getting the wrong people off is essential for your team, and company, to move forward and cultivate a culture of excellence with grit and work engagement at the forefront. So the question is: how do we become engaged in our work so when we use our grit our performance is enhanced? Well, it starts with identifying if your values and purpose align with that of the company's. If they do, identify others on the team who feel the same. If you find yourself around others who align with your values and purpose but still feel like you are not fully engaged in your work, then perhaps it has nothing to do with the values and has more to do with the level of grit you are surrounded with. As I mentioned earlier, passion without perseverance means you will become less engaged, you won't see results, and your effort will dwindle. This is where the Global G.R.I.T. System™ I talk about in the next chapter is crucial to teach you the elements that make up grit and how you can create habits of grit, not just for you, but for those around you.

Myth: If I combine my perseverance with my passion, I will immediately go from comfort to growth.

Wrong. There are two major zones in between the comfort zone and growth zone that have to be achieved before growth can take place.

The four stages include:

1. Comfort zone
2. Fear zone
3. Learning zone
4. Growth zone

How do we get to the learning zone from the fear zone? We have to use the"R" (reframe thinking) and the "I" (impact others) in the Global G.R.I.T. System™ that I discuss in Chapter 7 and 8 of this book. But how do we prepare for the fear zone? We have to choose our grit. What if you chose something you didn't like to do, day in and day out, but the more you do it, the more you learn how to adapt and adjust to the situation, until you become comfortable with it? Start by doing one thing. One thing you find difficult. This could be: drinking a gallon of water a day, learning to say "no" to things that don't align with your values, learning a new skill, striking up a conversation with a stranger, speaking up in a meeting or group discussion, having difficult conversations with team members, giving constructive feedback, engaging in public speaking, or taking on a physical challenge. The list is endless.

Just remember, to become good at something, you practice. To become great at something, you persist. To become a legend at something, you innovate and impact others in a profound and lasting way. To lead with grit is to lead with fortitude. To lead with the Global G.R.I.T. System™ is to lead with innovation and impact.

Why It's Not Your Fault

Society wants you to believe that perseverance and determination are the sole factors for success and grit. The number of times I have had people say "you will burn out" because I have relentless grit is overwhelming. What they fail to understand is that they are more at risk of burnout than I am, owing to their not following the five pillars. As long as the five pillars are in your life, daily, and you take care of your hardware, your software will live longer, function at a superior level, and provide boundless energy to work at the pace you desire.

Research points out, The restriction of sleep appears to prevent the effective clearance of toxic waste from the system and impedes normal neuronal performance.[11] Which means cutting into your sleep to appear more productive is actually hurting you and impacting your ability to be productive, which will lead to burnout. Working longer hours is not what grit is about. Not giving up, getting tasks done, reframing how you think and look at a situation to see the positive rather than the negative to create innovative solutions and taking responsibility and ownership of your actions is what grit is about. Cardiovascular disease, cancer, and diabetes account for almost 70% of all deaths in the United States; these diseases share inflammation as a common link.[12] With this in mind, it is not grit that causes burnout or untimely deaths, but rather chronic inflammation as a result of not taking care of oneself through the five pillars mentioned earlier in this chapter.

Many have asked me how I do it all without burning out. That includes training every day, running a business, managing a team, traveling all over the world to speak, creating leadership programs, building workshops and traveling across the world to lead them, consulting with clients, coaching executives, grieving for my son, managing PTSD, being a mother to my living children, and being a wife. My answer is the five pillars, daily. There is no negotiation with them. I always ensure eight hours of sleep a night, I drink 1.5 gallons of water a day, I exercise every single day, sometimes twice a day if a fitness competition is arising, I eat clean (no processed foods), I eat a lot of protein, and I ensure I go out in the sun for at least 10 minutes, twice a day. These are good habits I have developed, which require discipline. But once you carry these habits out over an extended period, you'll notice how it becomes routine and it's part of the excellence you foster around you. It attracts like-minded individuals, it attracts others who want to learn how you did it. You will notice within 30 to 60 days the difference in your energy, your sharpness of mind, your ability to carry out the tasks in a matter of days that previously may have taken you months to complete.

One of my secrets is that I time block. I treat time as my greatest currency. It is greater than money to me. Time blocking not just for work purposes, but for your food intake, for your water intake, for your bathroom breaks, for your end of the day cut off point that's non-negotiable, for your sleep, for your 10 minutes twice a day in the sun. In doing so, you are taking care of the most important part of living, your hardware, because without it, your software won't work. I talked earlier about upgrading your computer. Well, you can't upgrade your own hardware, but you can upgrade your software through taking care of your hardware. It's called neuroplasticity, and it means rewiring your thought patterns through new experiences to create different neurons and build new networks.[13] We can continue to do this throughout our life, right up until we die. No matter how old or young you are, anyone is capable of rewiring their brain through neuroplasticity.[14] The greatest myth surrounding grit is that it is a grind. Grit is not a grind. But continuously pushing oneself without the five pillars WILL lead to burnout.

Apply the five pillars, believe you can, and disregard those who are not part of your culture of excellence. For they will work tirelessly to hunt you, when in reality, you are hunting them.

"Never give in—never, never, never, never, in nothing great or small, large or petty, never give in except to convictions of honour and good sense. Never yield to force; never yield to the apparently overwhelming might of the enemy."

Winston Churchill, 1941

10 Key Leadership Lessons From This Chapter:

- Look after your hardware (body), if you want your software to effectively work (brain).

- Relentless grit does not lead to burnout. Not following the five pillars leads to burnout. Remember them:

  1. Water intake (1 gallon)

  2. Nutrition (eat clean, no processed foods)

  3. Exercise daily (elevate your heart rate each day)

  4. Sleep (at least 7.5 hours or more)

  5. Sun exposure (a few minutes each day)

- Identify your own values and purpose before you identify the values and purpose of others.

- Grit is not innate. Grit can be taught to anyone that wants to learn.

- You cannot expect to leave your comfort zone and enter your growth zone without fear, pain, and uncertainty.

- When you feel fear, dig deeper, as the only way to exit is to come out the other side into your learning zone. If you run back to your comfort zone, you have failed. Try again. And keep trying. Don't give in, don't give up for then the enemy has won.

- To become good at something, you practice. To become great at something, you persist. To become a legend at something, you innovate.

- Surround yourself with excellence, every single day and call this your culture of excellence.

- Condition your mind the way you can condition your body. Those thinking habits become a part of you and a part of your DNA.

- Do one thing every day that is out of your comfort zone. And do it, consistently.

CHAPTER 4

G.R.I.T.
Through It™

"Giving everything you possibly have,
when you don't have enough to give."

"Irish" Micky Ward
Light Welterweight Champion

Grit Birthday

September 2, 2021 changed my perspective on the word grit forever. It created a January 1st feeling for me, every single day. Ever noticed how there is a dramatic shift in how one thinks on January 1st? Intentions are always high, but are the actions to follow? What if we approach every day like it is January 1st with each day ensuring we write out, read aloud, and take action on the goals we promise ourselves we will accomplish at the beginning of the year. What if we thought about it differently? Instead of promising ourselves to take action on our goals we said, "This is who I am. I am already living this way."

Grit is a Skill

In Chapter 2 I discussed my journey with how I became an athlete under the leadership of my friend, fellow athlete, and Special Operations Marine Raider, Jason France. When I discussed grit with Jason he made compelling points. He says, "Grit is a skill. By understanding techniques and procedures that are involved in the game of life and self development we can avoid getting punched in the face by life's adversities over and over." In other words, to avoid falling deeper and deeper into a dark hole each time adversities arise, whether it be in the workplace or outside, if we came prepared with a "tool bag" of knowledge surrounding how to grit through a difficult situation, our resilience to such adversity becomes more robust. Our skills and knowledge become enhanced. Jason defines grit as, "One's learned ability to connect their physical and mental forces to reiterate hard processes." He had to connect his physical and mental forces to reiterate hard processes when he was drafted by the Cincinnati Reds out of his senior year of high school for baseball, with the Milwaukee Brewers drafting him out of his first year of college. But he didn't make it, and had to leave a world that he had known for the majority of his life. He had to redefine who he was. He joined the United States Marine Corps a couple of years later after going through hard times since his departure from baseball, and became a Marine Raider. He was highly trained and specialized in conducting special operations missions. It shifted his thinking and created an environment for which he could learn new skills, continue on his journey of self development, and learn new habits in which it shifted his mindset and highlighted the processes he had to go through to help develop grit.

If We Shift Our Thinking, We Shift Our Habits

In life, you can't avoid adversity. You can't run away from it. You can't hide from it. It will find you in your personal life, in business, with friends, teammates, or any other part of your life. And when it does, ask yourself: are you ready? Every single one of us will suffer at some point in our lives. If you haven't faced adversity, you will at some point. I can assure you of that. So are you going to suffer on your terms by choosing which grit you want to implement or are you going to allow the grit to choose you, not be prepared, and be forever trying to climb out of the vortex of pain that the grit is putting you through because you weren't prepared and you thought was unnecessary?

You have a choice. Each one of us will suffer at some point in life. The suffering comes and you can choose to run away or the suffering comes and you choose to face the pain.

It isn't even about overcoming something at this point. When the storm comes, and it will, if it hasn't already, you don't just learn how to "get through it," you will learn how to "G.R.I.T. Through It™." If we allow our minds to control us by allowing it to tell us that we can try another day, then you have the power to allow your mind to control you to stop giving yourself excuses. It is a matter of training our brains to believe what we want it to believe, to show our brains what we are really capable of and to teach our brain what grit really means. Then it becomes part of us, ingrained in our DNA, and something we don't have to think about when times become tough, because we've had so much training outside of the arena that when we need to pull from it and use it in battle, we are prepared, we are ready, and we face it, head on.

What's worse? The fear of doing something or the fear of not doing something? Fear isn't tangible. Fear is something we allow our bodies and minds to feel. It's something we've taught ourselves from when we were a young child. Why do some people have phobias and others do not? Fear. Their brains received information that something was fearful, perhaps from something they observed, perhaps from not understanding something, perhaps from being told it was fear by somebody else and allowing their brain to believe that, perhaps from something happening that caused pain and thus created fear. We give up at that point. We don't want to face it again or put ourselves through unnecessary pain, so we stop. It's a survival instinct. But what if we can use it as a positive? What if we can break through that fear zone, and enter into the learning zone, which will ultimately push us into our growth zone? What then? The results could be unfathomable.

I have heard many people say to me, "You are okay the way you are," or, "You shouldn't work so hard, you should rest," or, "When do you ever have downtime?" The truth is, you can always be more if you desire to be. You can work as hard, as smart, as much as you want to, if it gets you closer to the results of what you strive for. Your downtime could be very different to someone else's downtime and that's okay! I have had many people say to me, "You never rest," and I reply, "Yes I do. I train hard every single day. That's my downtime." People then argue with me saying, "No, no, I mean rest." I reply again with, "That is rest." They stare at me strangely. I have to explain that it is a rest for my mind. It is rest for my thoughts, it is rest and downtime for my active brain. You see, rest doesn't necessarily mean physical. What rest means to one person could mean something totally different to another. My brain receives downtime during my physical workouts and that's where I continue to refine my grit. Because I don't have to think about anything else. All I have to think about is getting through my grueling task at hand using my grit and the discipline I have instilled to ensure I never give up and continue to push through no matter what, because it's not about me. It's about my teammates. It's about not letting anybody else down just because you don't feel like it or think it's perfectly okay to throw in the towel when the going gets tough. You will die on the battlefield with that mentality. We can shape, change, and mold our daily habits to reflect those that we want to accomplish, but it will take grit. More specifically, it will take grit developed through the Global G.R.I.T. System™.

Introducing the Four Pillars of the Global G.R.I.T. System™

Get it done
Reframe thinking
Impact others
Take responsibility

Each letter of the Global G.R.I.T. System™ is discussed in detail in Chapters 6 through 9 of this book.

There is a strong belief that in order to have grit one has to have passion and perseverance.[1] But what if we looked at it differently? I challenge this status quo and believe that everyone has grit. We have it as babies when we learn to crawl, then walk, we never give up and eventually learn how to do it, but over time we lose our ability to tap into it. As a result of their environment and the people they surround themselves with, people get stuck in a bubble where everyone thinks the norm is to not have the grit and those that do possess it are just born with it. Angela Duckworth, who carried out research in the subject of grit, explains that "Grit is having stamina, grit is sticking with your future and sticking at it for years and making that future a reality," but when asked how one can build grit, she did not have the answer. Carol Dweck came up with the theory of a "growth mindset".[2] Angela Duckworth points out that perhaps having a growth mindset is what builds grit. Even then, having a growth mindset in which one's ability to learn is not fixed, but can be changed,[3] is not enough.

Motivation shapes what we think, and thus affects our cognition.[4] Our cognition affects our brain processes, and brain processes are affected by our ability to adopt a growth mindset.[5] We have to have the motivation to adopt a growth mindset for it to work. What motivates individuals? Belief. What empowers individuals? Belief. What helps in decision-making? Belief. How do we create that belief? Awareness. It is science. Our biochemistry is belief-reinforced awareness. It all stems from our ability to believe we can, and we will. Each and every cell in our body is aware of our thoughts and feelings, which means our cells are also aware of our beliefs.[6] These beliefs shape our perception and understanding of the world around us, influencing our awareness and experiences.

So, the question is, what creates the belief? Our environment and knowledge. Past experiences also create our belief,[7] but what if past beliefs caused failure, and those with a fixed mindset give up as a result of those past experiences? Thus, past experiences are not necessary to create belief. Maybe they are in part for those that already possess a growth mindset, but for those that have a fixed mindset, past negative experiences do not help them. So let's focus on the environment and knowledge. The environment is in your control. You decide who you want to be around and have in your culture of excellence as discussed in prior chapters. The knowledge part is where many are stuck. Until now. Until the Global G.R.I.T. System™.

Research has discovered the importance of providing autonomy over student learning to enhance self-regulation, especially as effort, motivation, and resilience are impacted by a growth mindset.[8] In doing so, this will have a direct impact on students' motivation to learn subjects at school instead of depending on the assumption that students are interested in learning.

Now let's relate that to the workplace, for not just ourselves, but our employees, and in our adult life. What if we gave the knowledge of the Global G.R.I.T. System™ to our team members, employees, those around us, and provided an environment in which they had the autonomy to apply this knowledge in all aspects of their life and facilitated an environment in which they could use this firsthand knowledge without being told how and when to use it? In doing so, we provide the awareness to them in which we give them the knowledge while providing the environment, which in turn creates the belief, providing the motivation, which influences our cognition, altering our brain processes, providing the positive attitude which leads to the adoption of the growth mindset to apply the Global G.R.I.T. System™ in every single avenue of life.

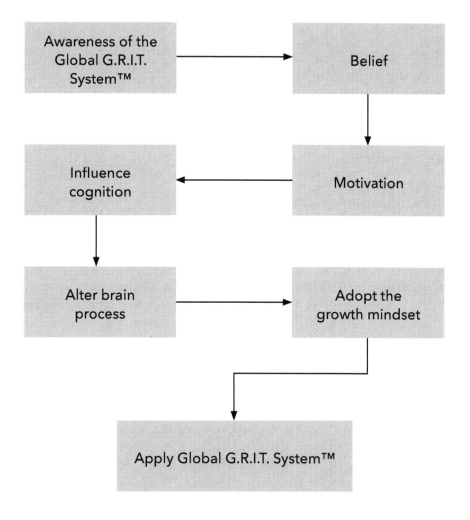

Here's a few examples of situations in which you can use the Global G.R.I.T. System™:

- **Bounce back from a bad quarter:** G.R.I.T. Through It™
- **Resolve, manage, and avoid team conflict:** G.R.I.T. Through It™
- **Manage market volatility and economic downturns:** G.R.I.T. Through It™
- **Develop a culture of excellence through mergers and acquisitions:** G.R.I.T. Through It™

- **Gain, train, and retain top talent:** G.R.I.T. Through It™
- **Performance through adversity:** G.R.I.T. Through It™
- **Recover quickly from funding and investment challenges:** G.R.I.T. Through It™
- **Performance through challenging times:** G.R.I.T. Through It™
- **Navigate political uncertainty:** G.R.I.T. Through It™

You get the idea. No matter what issue or problem you face, you can use the Global G.R.I.T. System™ to grit through any situation. It provides the knowledge for you to create the environment you need to harness the system of grit, and apply it practically. The Global G.R.I.T. System™ will become the good habits you need in order to carry out the tasks you have to accomplish to achieve your goals. In Chapter 2, I discussed my journey to becoming an athlete and passing the standard. Well passing that grueling fitness test meant more than just getting to train with the elites. It meant I put the tragedy of my son's death and my own near death experience into something that had great meaning: to show others what can be possible when you G.R.I.T. Through It™.

The Global G.R.I.T. System™, when applied, will become part of your DNA and transform the way you lead, both in and outside of the workplace, impacting everyone around you, unequivocally.

"Life doesn't happen to us,
it happens because of us."

Jason France

10 Key Leadership Lessons From This Chapter:

- Identify your grit birthday, recognize it, and remind yourself of it, every single day.

- Grit is a skill that can be taught and developed. Shift your thinking and you'll shift your habits.

- Fear isn't tangible. Fear is something we allow our bodies and minds to feel.

- Rest doesn't necessarily mean physical. Resting your mind versus resting your body. What rest means to one person could mean something totally different to another.

- The four pillars of the Global G.R.I.T. System™:
    - **G**et it Done
    - **R**eframe Thinking
    - **I**mpact others
    - **T**ake Responsibility

- Understand that grit is a process applied through the Global G.R.I.T. System™.

- Everyone has grit. We just need to use the four pillars of the Global G.R.I.T. System™ to learn how to tap into it.

- Change starts with belief. Knowledge and environment create belief. So provide the knowledge of the Global G.R.I.T. System™ and create the environment for your team members to provide the autonomy to apply the Global G.R.I.T. System™, which creates the belief.

- Our biochemistry (the chemical processes and reactions that occur within us) is belief-reinforced awareness (shapes our perception and understanding of the world around us). We need awareness of the Global G.R.I.T. System™ to have belief. We need belief to provide motivation. We need motivation to influence our cognition. We need cognition to alter our brain process. We need our brain process to create the positive attitude to adopt the growth mindset. We need the growth mindset to apply the Global G.R.I.T. System™

- Adopt the Global G.R.I.T. System™ in every single avenue of life, from leadership in the workplace to leadership at home. Review the "G.R.I.T. Through It™" examples in this chapter. Take a look at your workplace and identify the areas which need the most attention and look at implementing the Global G.R.I.T. System™ to G.R.I.T. Through It™.

CHAPTER 5

The Global
G.R.I.T. System™

---

*"The Global G.R.I.T. System™ is not just
a corporate tool or a workplace tool,
it is a societal tool."*

Anthony Mirabile
Managing Director, Asset and Wealth
Management Division, Goldman Sachs

The Transformative Power of the Global G.R.I.T. System™

The Global G.R.I.T. System™ not only helps you conquer challenges, like climbing mountains you see ahead, it also redefines the landscape for others by shifting the very plateaus, elevating not just yourself but those who follow your trail. It raises the bar and sets a new standard, resulting in a culture of excellence and a team full of hunters who are prepared in all elements of grit and ready at the first sign of adversity. By adopting the Global G.R.I.T. System™, you're not just leading—you're transforming. Whether you're an individual seeking personal excellence, a team member aspiring to elevate others, or a leader aiming to leave an indelible impact, the Global G.R.I.T. System™ serves as your blueprint for unparalleled achievement. Don't just aim to be good, commit to being gritty. Because it's the grit you harness through the Global G.R.I.T. System™ that turns potential into performance, trials into triumphs, and aspirations into actualizations. With the Global G.R.I.T. System™ you don't just aim for the sky, you reach for the stars. You evolve from a lion surviving the wilderness to the lion that reshapes the terrain, opening new horizons for your pride. The system instills the techniques to prepare and cultivate a tool bag to develop all areas of grit and provide the confidence, belief, and motivation to help know when to pull from which grit pillar to get you through any situation.

PART 1:
The Framework of the Four Pillars
of the Global G.R.I.T. System™

Get it Done
Reframe Thinking
Impact Others
Take Responsibility

Grit is a skill that can be taught as a result of the Global G.R.I.T. System™, but the four pillars are a framework built around a set of behaviors that create the skills needed to establish the foundation for building, developing, and advancing performance to amplify success in leadership.

I had the pleasure of interviewing my friend, Anthony Mirabile, Managing Director of the Asset and Wealth Management division at Goldman Sachs, who has been with Goldman Sachs for 23 years in a variety of leadership positions. Anthony told me, "Leadership is not a skill. Leadership is a behavior." Let's think about that for a moment. So frequently, organizations are focused on teaching the "skills" of leadership. What if we thought about it differently? In Chapter 3 of this book I discussed how awareness of something creates the belief, that in turn creates the motivation that influences cognition and alters the brain processes. That in turn provides the positive attitude necessary to adopt the growth mindset, which allows one to apply the very thing that they became aware of in the first place. The Global G.R.I.T. System™ will help you develop the behaviors required for long-term advancement so you can establish and apply the skills outlined in the four pillars of the Global G.R.I.T. System™ framework. Without that, you won't be able to retain the leadership skills you learn. We need to switch our focus from thinking of leadership as a skill and instead understanding leadership as a behavior. This is what the four pillars of the Global G.R.I.T. System™ is designed to do.

The Framework Behind the Global G.R.I.T. System™

I believe, based on my experience and educational background, there are four key components of leadership: accountability, communication, emotional Intelligence, and decision-making. I've used these components to develop leadership programs. Anthony Mirabile pointed out to me that they are also the building blocks of the Global G.R.I.T. System™ framework. In other words, each essential attribute of leadership can be attributed to the behaviors that create the framework of the Global G.R.I.T. System™. Let's take a closer look.

The "G" in the Global G.R.I.T. System™ = "Get It Done"

To get it done means to take action with urgency. It means to complete a task to accomplish a particular objective. How do we do this? We have to believe we can, first and foremost. Most people give up and either don't end up finishing what they started or don't start at all because they don't believe they can get it done. If they had the belief, they would have the motivation. Without motivation, they can't influence their cognition. If they can't influence their cognition, they can't alter their brain process, which means they remain in a fixed mindset and don't adopt the growth mindset. Micky Ward says, "Tomorrow never comes," and Anthony Mirabile takes that even further, saying, "Tomorrow is for weak-minded individuals." Two fierce, extremely successful leaders in their own field. What is the common denominator between the two? Taking action to get it done. Grit requires action. Getting it done, no matter the circumstance. The discussion of how to "get it done," with techniques, can be found in Chapter 6 of this book.

The "R" in the Global G.R.I.T. System™ = "Reframe Thinking"

Reframing thinking is shifting our perspective and allowing our thought process to identify multiple ways to view a situation, regardless of the positives or negatives. This can be an extremely challenging portion of the Global G.R.I.T. System™ framework and probably the one that will require the most practice to achieve as a daily habit. We are hardwired to have a negativity bias and focus immediately on the negatives of situations and identify problems as a result, without realizing the positives and solutions immediately.[1] When problems arise or situations occur that we feel we don't have control over, we tend to focus on interventions.[2] However, interventions are purely just the instruments we use. In order to identify the right instrument to use, we first have to identify the root cause of why the intervention is needed in the first place. It stems back to the role of cognition in the emotions we express and is one of the oldest subjects of discussion in psychology.[3]

Many view emotions as a negative trait, but emotions are actually a power source if we know how to use them correctly and adapt them, over time, to provide an advantage.[4] If we could choose the emotion before it chose us, meaning we use cognition to control emotion, we could very easily gain control of our thoughts, put them up on a whiteboard and look at it from all angles, using a logical standpoint. We have to understand and be aware of the science behind reframing how we look at situations, and reframing how we think. This creates a belief in what we do, which creates motivation, which influences cognition, which alters the brain process to provide the positive attitude to adopt the growth mindset and create a habit out of it. We are rewiring our brain, rewiring our thinking, shifting our perspective, and opening up our minds to the realm of possibilities to change the way we look at situations, regardless if they are positive or negative, ultimately instilling grit. Chapter 7 details how to apply the "reframe thinking" technique.

The "I" in the Global G.R.I.T. System™ = "Impact Others"

Impacting others, as a leader, means to influence, inspire, guide, motivate, and empower individuals *within* your team and *as* a team. In doing so, this will help to reveal their full potential, foster their growth, and create a purposeful difference in their lives, ultimately contributing to the collective success within the organization.

Innovation is crucial for companies to develop and thrive while remaining competitive in a fast-paced, dynamic, ever-changing landscape.[5] However, what creates the foundation for organizational innovation are the individuals within the organization.[6] Thus, the innovative behavior of employees has a positive influence on the company's performance. So how do companies inspire the innovation within their team members? Leadership. It is critical that leaders impact others within their team and organization to directly and indirectly influence employees' behavior by demonstrating innovative behavior themselves.[7]

It comes back to providing the environment for team members to have autonomy and thrive, which leads to the belief, and in turn leads to the motivation that influences their cognition. This then impacts their brain processes, and they adopt the growth mindset to apply the very innovation that was created through the process I just described. By empowering their team in this way, and impacting others, individuals will recognize and feel the support and attention from the company, which will ultimately lead to innovative behavior.[8] This leads to increased competitiveness, enhanced performance, heightened productivity, development of new products or services, and an environment of creativity and a culture of excellence, and instills grit. I discuss further, in Chapter 8, the ways impacting others can be achieved to act as an aid to develop grit within your team.

The "T" in the Global G.R.I.T. System™ = "Take Responsibility"

Take responsibility for your decisions, own actions, lack of action, lack of decision, and understand that there are consequences, positive or negative, to every choice you make. Holding oneself accountable for those decisions and actions is critical when taking responsibility. This means owning up to your mistakes, taking the initiative to resolve issues, and being proactive as well as creative in finding solutions. Do not blame others for a situation that has not transpired in the way you had hoped. It starts with you. Don't be soft on others, but don't be soft on yourself, either. Take responsibility for your situation and for your own actions. What you do doesn't just affect you, it affects those around you. So if it's not serving you, it's not serving others. How you are affected by what you do, daily, the decisions you make, and the decisions you don't make, also affects those around you. So if you are unsure about making the change for you, then don't. Make it for others instead. Take ownership for making that change for others. Put your team before yourself. In leadership we come up against challenges like this often. Having to make uncomfortable decisions, not just for you, but for your team. You can't get away from tough decisions in leadership, but you can get away from poor decisions. Don't let the inaction of others be the inaction of you. Take responsibility. Own it. Change it.

Over the past 40 years, Americans have increased their average caloric intake by 12 percent, yet they also have become more sedentary, leading to obesity.[9] Obesity did not happen because of high caloric foods, it happened because the individual chose to make the decision to consume such high calorie foods and they chose not to be active in order to maintain a healthy lifestyle.[10] Individuals who often lack accountability blame others for their actions.[11] Blame can also be attributed to fear. Because of the fear, it can go against what we think is true about what's being blamed and what we believe should be true about the person doing the blaming.[12] These individuals may also have a fixed mindset, which hinders the development of grit.[13] Consequently, taking responsibility is a major component for achieving and developing grit. Techniques and types of responsibility are discussed in Chapter 9 of this book.

PART 2:
The Process of Adopting
the Global G.R.I.T. System™

In Chapter 4 of this book I talked about how motivation shapes what we think, and therefore affects our cognition. In turn, our cognition affects our brain processes, and brain processes are affected by our ability to adopt a growth mindset. In order to adopt a growth mindset, we have to have the motivation to do so. In order to feel motivated, we need to have belief. In order for the belief to be created, one has to have awareness, either through visual stimuli, education, or they see someone else do it. All of this is science. I stated in the previous chapter that our biochemistry is belief-reinforced awareness.[14] In order to adopt a process we have to believe we can. Our beliefs influence our experiences, which influence our perception and understanding of everything around us.

Autonomy is paramount to the importance of adopting a growth mindset, and having a growth mindset forms part of the process of being able to apply the Global G.R.I.T. System™. Having the autonomy and creating the environment in which others have that autonomy is critical for developing motivation to adopt the process.

Here is a visual of the Global G.R.I.T. System™ process necessary to adopt the Global G.R.I.T. System™.

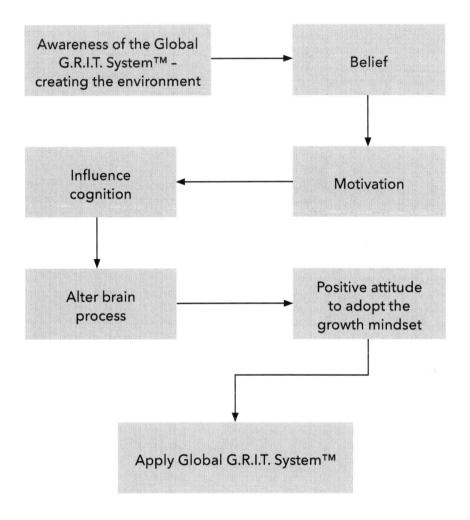

Adopting the Global G.R.I.T. System™ doesn't happen overnight. It is a process. By creating the environment for your team to become aware of the Global G.R.I.T. System™, and what it can achieve for each individual and the organization as a whole, you will help them create the belief that they can develop grit, even if grit hasn't chosen them at any point in their life. It addresses the myths surrounding grit and changes their belief system to show them that anyone can develop grit by following the Global G.R.I.T. System™. With this new belief surrounding grit, you will create the motivation in individuals and teams to want to do something about it, which influences their cognition directly. When their cognition is impacted in this way, it changes brain patterns and alters the way we think. Then one's brain processes start to modify and adapt. Altering brain processes leads to a positive attitude to adopt a "growth mindset".[15] A growth mindset is needed in order to understand that one's ability to learn is not "fixed" and regardless of past experiences and background, anyone can learn and develop grit and apply it to any setting they choose. This leads to applying the Global G.R.I.T. System™, thus accepting that grit can be taught and most certainly developed in anyone.

PART 3:
The Four Types of the Global G.R.I.T. System™

As part of the Global G.R.I.T. System™, it is important to recognize your own as well as others' strengths in grit and areas for improvement, as defined by the four pillars that make up the framework of the Global G.R.I.T. System™, which I explained at the beginning of this chapter. Now let's look at the four types of grit. You will be dominant in one specific area of the four grit types, below:

1. Go-Getter
2. Reframer
3. Innovator
4. Trustworthy Titan

To identify which "grit type" you are dominant in and identify the level of grit you have in the other areas, and understand where your strengths lay and where areas of improvement are needed, you can take the "grit type indicator" assessment (introduced later in this chapter).

The Characteristics of a Go-Getter

Go-getters are the ones who don't wait for something to happen, they make it happen. They take initiative and are self-motivated to pursue the goals they set out to achieve. They are self-starters who have a very clear focus about the direction they are heading and are extremely disciplined individuals. As such, they are effective with their time management and they believe in their abilities and have the confidence to take calculated risks when necessary. They perform under pressure and easily adapt to situations and the environment around them. They are extremely competitive and driven, measuring progress and attaining tangible outcomes. As such, go-getters take action, pursue their goals, and consistently achieve results. They do what needs to be done, they don't put it off, and are task-oriented individuals. They turn ideas into action and thrive on autonomy and having different choices to make their own decisions. They have a strong work ethic and carry out tasks in order of importance.

These characteristics enable go-getters to take action, pursue their goals, and consistently achieve results. I talk more about how to develop these characteristics in Chapter 6.

Examples of Go-Getters include:

Michael Jordan: Michael Jordan had an incredible work ethic, always looking to improve his skills. He had a tremendous competitive drive. His relentless drive to win and ability to perform under high-pressure situations, such as shooting a game-winning shot with seconds to go when the series was tied in the 1998 NBA finals, securing the championship for the Chicago Bulls, is further evidence of his ability to focus on the task at hand, and deliver when it mattered the most.

"If you quit once it becomes a habit. Never quit!"
Michael Jordan

Sir Richard Branson: Founder of the Virgin Group, and owner of over 400 companies through the Virgin Group, he is renowned for his entrepreneurial spirit, risk-taking, and adaptability in environments to create and turn ideas into successful endeavors.

"You don't learn to walk by following rules.
You learn by doing, and by falling over."
Sir Richard Branson

Winston Churchill: His refusal to surrender to Nazi Germany, even in the face of overwhelming odds and severe pressure, showed his determination. He also did not waste any time to build alliances with other nations to ensure victory in the war. This demonstrated his adaptability, willingness to take risks, tenacity, and handling of tasks in order of importance. He did not shy away from making difficult decisions.

> *"Never give in, never give in, never, never, never,*
> *never—in nothing, great or small, large or petty—*
> *never give in except to convictions of honour and*
> *good sense. Never yield to force; never yield to the*
> *apparently overwhelming might of the enemy."*
> Winston Churchill

The Characteristics of a Reframer

A reframer is someone who actively engages in the process of reframing their thoughts. They have the ability to change their perspective, reinterpret situations, and find new ways of thinking about things. A reframer will shift their mindset and view challenges or circumstances from a different angle. They are problem solvers. They are logical and make decisions based on that logic. They need time to think and look for patterns and connections, and are known for being incredibly knowledgeable. They are critical thinkers and have multiple perspectives on situations. They analyze situations and are always finding new solutions rather than problems and have a positive mindset. They see situations from different perspectives and challenge assumptions, offering alternative interpretations by taking into account many lessons they have learned in the past. They are excellent thinkers and extremely committed to their process.

These characteristics enable reframers to find new ways to approach problems, think outside the box, and help others to see situations from different angles. I will discuss how to develop the characteristics of a reframer in Chapter 7.

Examples of Reframers include:

Chris Gardner: The 2006 movie *The Pursuit of Happyness* highlighted Chris Gardner's story of how he reframed his thinking even when times were extremely tough and he ended up sleeping in a public bathroom with his young son. Instead of letting his circumstances define him, he reframed his thinking and was grateful to have a roof over his head, even if it was a public bathroom. He could lock the door and know he and his son were safe, and used the small amount of cash he had to buy food to feed his son and himself. By reframing how he thought about his situation, and maintaining a positive mindset, he was able to overcome adversity by changing the way he looked at situations and never giving up until he found an answer. He was committed to the process to get to where he needed to be.

> *"One of the things young people always ask me about is what is the secret to success. The secret is there is no secret. It's the basics. Blocking and tackling."*
> **Chris Gardner**

Roger Bannister: The first person to run a mile in under four minutes. He was told, as were many others, that it was physically impossible for a human to run a mile in under four minutes. Instead of accepting that as final, he looked at it differently and found solutions to the problem for other runners. He focused on his running technique and endurance and was determined to push the boundaries of what was thought to be physically possible. He reframed how he thought, which impacted the thoughts of others and reframed how they approached the four minute mile, and suddenly others were able to run a mile in under four minutes.

> *"Just because they say it's impossible, doesn't mean you can't do it."*
> **Roger Bannister**

Sara Blakely: The founder of Spanx, Sara approached the fashion industry with a very different view and found a solution to a problem for many women through shapewear that changed the shape of a woman's body under clothing. She challenged the status quo and thought differently to disrupt a billion dollar industry, demonstrating her ability to change not only her own perspective in relation to fashion, but the perspective of millions of others.

*"Don't be intimidated by what you don't know.
That can be your greatest strength and ensure that
you do things differently from everyone else."*
Sara Blakely

The Characteristics of an Innovator

An innovator is a person who is creative, forward-thinking, and who introduces new ideas to improve a particular field of interest. They are divergent thinkers, inspirational and motivating. They have incredible imaginations, are visionaries, have boundless energy, and can paint a picture for others. They love to brainstorm, are optimistic, and they find it easy to put thoughts, ideas, actions, and feelings into words. They see the possibilities, and are excellent at promoting collaboration and innovation within a team by creating an environment that motivates individuals to work together toward a common goal and achieve outstanding results. Innovators have a curious mind, a willingness to take risks, and the ability to think outside the box. They look to bring about positive change in others through new ideas and approaches and their actions and words have a lasting influence on others. They are driven to turn their ideas into tangible innovations that can make a positive impact across the board.

These characteristics enable innovators to think creatively, generate new ideas, create the belief in others, challenge conventional thinking, and find unique solutions to problems. They are able to see opportunities where others may not. Techniques to develop the characteristics of an innovator are discussed in Chapter 8.

Examples of Innovators include:

Steve Jobs: Co-founder and creator of Apple Inc., developer of smartphones, digital music, and computers. He had a visionary mindset, the ability to think differently and impact the world with groundbreaking products that revolutionized industries.

"Innovation distinguishes between a leader and a follower."
Steve Jobs

Usain Bolt: An Olympian and world champion sprinter, he is known for his exceptional speed and ability to captivate and influence others. His innovative approach to sprinting, his training methods, and unique running style has influenced the field of athletics and inspired future generations of sprinters.

> *"One thing I've learned over the years is that if you don't believe in yourself, no one will do it for you."*
> Usain Bolt

Marie Curie: Polish-born physicist and chemist who later became a French citizen. She was known for her pioneering research on radioactivity, which led to the discovery of two elements, polonium and radium. Her work revolutionized the understanding of radioactivity and laid the foundation for advancements in nuclear physics and medical treatments. She won a Nobel Prize in two different scientific fields (physics and chemistry).

> *"Nothing in life is to be feared, it is only to be understood. Now is the time to understand more, so that we may fear less."*
> Marie Curie

The Characteristics of a Trustworthy Titan

A Trustworthy Titan is a person who is people-oriented, reliable, and likable. They create trust by having good follow-through and creating powerful relationships with others. They are great negotiators, can see both sides of a situation, and appreciate the differences in others.

They can see points of view that people have in common, they are dependable and consistent. They are fair and just in their treatment of others and own up to their own actions and accept the consequences of their choices. They have a strong sense of duty toward their responsibilities and are incredibly loyal and patient. They have an instinctive understanding of others and they sense what it is like to be someone else. They often have deep relationships within a small circle. They believe everyone is equally important and valued, and they like to help others experience success. They have an understanding and consider the needs and perspectives of others. They have a strong sense of purpose in life, and they can see how people who are very different can work together and can see points of view that people have in common. They are accountable and will ensure others are held accountable, too.

These characteristics enable Trustworthy Titans to gain the trust of others and enable their team to rely on them to fulfill their responsibilities. I discuss how to develop the characteristics of a Trustworthy Titan in Chapter 9.

Examples of Trustworthy Titans include:

Abraham Lincoln: Abraham Lincoln was known for his honesty, integrity, and strong moral character, making him an incredible trustworthy titan. An example of his trustworthiness was when he took ownership of the Emancipation Proclamation and took responsibility for issuing the executive order that declared enslaved individuals in the Confederacy territory to be free. Despite facing severe criticism, Lincoln stood by his decision and took responsibility for his actions.

> *"I am not bound to win, but I am bound to be true. I am not bound to succeed, but I am bound to live up to what light I have."*
> **Abraham Lincoln**

Malala Yousafzai: A Pakistani activist and Nobel laureate, Malala gained international recognition by advocating for girls' education and women's rights specifically in her native Swat Valley in Pakistan, where the Taliban had banned girls from attending school. She took responsibility for her actions and survived an assassination attempt by the Taliban, in 2012, and continues to work tirelessly to promote education and empower young girls around the world.

> *"I raise up my voice not so I can shout, but so that those without a voice can be heard."*
> **Malala Yousafzai**

Eleanor Roosevelt: First Lady of the United States of America from 1933 to 1945, Eleanor was known for her compassion and dedication to improving the lives of others by playing an active role in shaping public policy. She championed the cause of African American rights, supported the work of civil rights activists, and pushed for anti-lynching legislation. She demonstrated integrity, empathy, and transparency, as she understood the needs and perspectives of different individuals and communities, enabling her to advocate for their rights and well-being.

"We shape our lives, and we shape ourselves.
The process never ends until we die. And the choices
we make are ultimately our own responsibility."
Eleanor Roosevelt

The Grit Type Indicator™

The Grit Type Indicator™ is a groundbreaking assessment tool I have developed and it's the key element of the comprehensive Global G.R.I.T. System™. Drawing inspiration from well-established personality and behavioral evaluations, this tool functions as a thorough psychometric instrument in the context of "grit." While every individual possesses traits from all four pillars in the Global G.R.I.T. System™, the Grit Type Indicator™ identifies your dominant "grit type" and also ranks the remaining types in a specific sequence based on your unique grit strength. This allows you to understand your primary grit strength, whether it's as a "Go-Getter," "Reframer," "Innovator," or "Trustworthy Titan," while also revealing which areas follow in descending order of strength. This layered insight is invaluable, as it enables you to pinpoint where you excel, which grit type is your secondary strength, and which areas require further development for a well-rounded grit profile. The Global G.R.I.T. System™ includes a range of tools and strategies designed to strengthen your non-dominant grit traits, as well as amplifying the capabilities of your primary grit type.

How it works:

- **Psychometric Assessment:** Participants undergo a thorough assessment of carefully designed questions that measure their inclinations and capabilities in each of the four pillars of grit.

- **Scoring and Categorization:** Scores from the assessment are then categorized into one of four "grit types" that is more dominant and at the core of behavior and decision-making:
  - Go-Getters: Individuals who excel in taking action and getting things done.
  - Reframers: Those who are adept at viewing challenges as opportunities and can change the narrative.
  - Innovators: Creative thinkers who bring fresh, groundbreaking ideas to the table.
  - Trustworthy Titans: The bedrock of any team or organization, they are accountable, reliable, and uphold high ethical standards.
- **Personalized Insights:** Based on the results, individuals receive an in-depth report, providing insights into their strengths, areas for improvement, and recommendations for how to employ their specific "grit type" in various scenarios.
- **Team Dynamics:** When administered across a team or organization, the Grit Type Indicator™ can be used to identify if you have the right people in the right seats, reveal potential gaps in grit, and offer strategies to achieve a balanced, high-performing team.
- **Action Plans:** By recognizing their grit type, individuals and teams can then formulate action plans with the help of the Global G.R.I.T. System™ to drive change and deliver results.
- **Evolutionary Tool:** What sets the Grit Type Indicator™ apart is its focus on continual improvement. As individuals or organizations evolve, they can retake the assessment to measure their growth, adapt their strategies accordingly, and view their progress.

The Grit Type Indicator™ is not a personality assessment—it's a transformative instrument that offers actionable intelligence to help individuals and organizations harness the power of grit, thereby impacting society and creating a paradigm shift for leaders and others. While every individual possesses traits from all four pillars, the assessment is designed to identify one dominant "grit type" that shapes the core of their behavior and decision-making.

The Breakdown of the Grit Type Indicator™

- **Holistic View:** The Grit Type Indicator™ understands that individuals are complex and multi-faceted. While the assessment categorizes people into one of four primary "grit types," it also acknowledges and measures the sub-dominant traits that everyone possesses.

- **Dominant Trait Identification:** Through comprehensive evaluation, the tool pinpoints which of the four pillars is the most dominant in an individual. This serves as the "North Star" for their grit-centric behavior and actions.

- **Balanced Skill Sets:** While the dominant trait plays a pivotal role, the presence of sub-dominant traits ensures a more balanced skill set. For example, a "Go-Getter" might also have a strong "Innovator" streak, bringing a unique blend of action and creativity to the table.

- **Harmonizing Teams:** When employed organization-wide, the Grit Type Indicator™ can identify the dominant and sub-dominant traits within a team, allowing for a harmonious blend of skills and attributes that fosters synergy and elevates performance.

- **Personal Development Plans:** With insights into their dominant and sub-dominant traits, individuals can craft targeted development plans that leverage their primary strengths while also nurturing their less dominant attributes.

- **Dynamic Adaptability:** Recognizing that grit types are not static and can evolve over time, the Grit Type Indicator™ can be retaken periodically to track shifts in dominant and sub-dominant traits, making it an invaluable tool for ongoing personal and professional development.

By identifying not just the dominant trait but also appreciating the blend of all four, your Grit Type Indicator™ offers a richer, more holistic view of grit. This allows for more nuanced strategies for personal growth, team development, and organizational success and allows you to see how others see you.

Introducing the G.R.I.T. Quadrant™

The G.R.I.T. Quadrant™ serves as a foundational component within the Global G.R.I.T. System™ for its ability to offer immediate, actionable insights into an individual's grit profile. Think of it as your grit "compass", guiding you toward understanding your instinctive reactions to adversity and scenarios requiring resilience, focus, and drive. It sorts individuals into one of four distinct zones: Logical, Intuitive, Energetic, and Reserved. It also offers a snapshot of where one naturally gravitates when grit is most needed. While it provides an excellent starting point, its real power comes from how seamlessly it integrates with the more comprehensive Grit Type Indicator™. Together, they form a complete toolkit for personal and organizational grit development, making the G.R.I.T. Quadrant™ an indispensable part of the Global G.R.I.T. System™.

The G.R.I.T. Quadrant™ measures a "Cognitive Axis," which measures grit thought processes and grit problem-solving styles, and "Temperament Axis," measuring grit demeanor and grit approach to situations that require action or restraint. It maps your grit tendencies along two axes: Logical-Intuitive and Energetic-Reserved. If you find yourself as a Logical and Energetic individual, you'll naturally gravitate toward the "Go-getter" category, embodying the "G" in the Global G.R.I.T. System™. These are the people who approach challenges head-on, always eager for action. On the other hand, if you're Logical but Reserved, the "Reframer" or "R" type is likely your dominant grit trait. These individuals excel at seeing problems from new angles and finding creative solutions within established boundaries. Those who are Intuitive and Energetic align most closely with the "I" or "Innovator" type. These are the individuals who thrive in uncertainty, using their intuition to find new paths and inspire those around them. Finally, if you're more of an Intuitive and Reserved person, you'll find your dominant grit in the "T" category: "Take Responsibility." These are individuals who are highly introspective, who consider the larger picture and take ownership of their actions and decisions.

The G.R.I.T. Quadrant™ serves as a quick reference for identifying the behavioral tendencies most relevant in scenarios that call for specific dimensions of grit. Say, for instance, you're navigating a situation where the "T" (Take Responsibility) in the Global G.R.I.T. System™ is crucial. In such cases, channeling your Reserved and Intuitive traits becomes the priority. To fully elevate and diversify your grit capabilities, it's beneficial to engage with all four sectors of the G.R.I.T. Quadrant™.

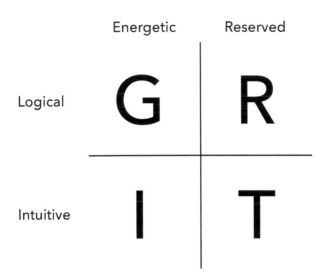

The Power of the G.R.I.T. Quadrant™

The brilliance of the quadrant lies in its elegant simplicity, paired with profound depth. It offers immediate insight into your dominant grit tendencies; whether you're a Go-Getter, Reframer, Innovator, or Trustworthy Titan. This quadrant is the product of rigorous research and deep psychological understanding. It lays the groundwork for targeted development and transformative growth. However, while the G.R.I.T. Quadrant™ serves as an indispensable compass to identify your dominant grit trait, it's the Grit Type Indicator™ that offers the full-depth assessment. This advanced tool dives deep into your grit type, revealing not just your dominant trait but also your secondary and tertiary traits, providing a comprehensive understanding of your strengths and areas for improvement within all four pillars of grit.

The Global G.R.I.T. Quadrant™ is simple to grasp yet impactful in its revelations, and is a stepping stone to the more comprehensive insights provided by the Grit Type Indicator™.

PART 4:
Putting it All Together: The System

Together, the pillars, the process, and the types of grit make up the system of developing grit. The Global G.R.I.T. System™ cultivates the growth and resilience of an individual while strengthening the areas in which they are strong and identifying the areas where they need to improve, while providing the tools to succeed.

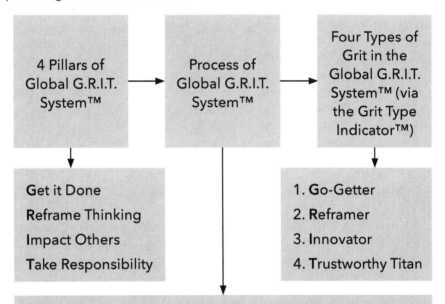

4 Pillars of Global G.R.I.T. System™ → Process of Global G.R.I.T. System™ → Four Types of Grit in the Global G.R.I.T. System™ (via the Grit Type Indicator™)

Get it Done

Reframe Thinking

Impact Others

Take Responsibility

1. Go-Getter

2. Reframer

3. Innovator

4. Trustworthy Titan

1. Create the awareness of the Global G.R.I.T. System™ – enable the environment for visual, auditory and practical learners.

2. Establishes the belief that they can develop grit.

3. Generates the motivation for the individual to want to actively engage and participate.

4. Influences cognition.

5. Alters brain processes and patterns.

6. Initiates a willingness to adopt a "growth mindset."

7. Leads to the application of the Global G.R.I.T. System™

When you understand the framework of the Global G.R.I.T. System™ and use the practical examples discussed in Chapters 6 to 9 of this book, it will change you as an individual and as a leader, including the way you look at your team and others around you. So simple yet so profound. When you educate your team with the four pillars of the Global G.R.I.T. System™, people who feel less "gritty" than others and those who believe they have "grittiness" are able to enhance their areas of strength. By taking the Grit Type Indicator™ you will see that you and every single one of your team members has a certain level of grit. It is important for you, as the leader, to identify which grit type they are (through having them take the assessment), so you are in a better position to ensure you have the right people in the right roles. This isn't just about pleasing everyone on the team. You can't please everyone. You will lose respect if you try. It's not a good day for any leader if that happens. Thus, by identifying which "grit type" your team members are, you are able to build a powerhouse of a team in all areas of the business. Your team will also feel valued and recognized for their strengths, which you may not have known they had if you defined grit as having passion and perseverance alone. In developing the Global G.R.I.T. System™, I have created a structure to prepare a team of individuals to learn and better yet, apply grit. This can only be achieved by not skipping the process portion of the system, and starts by creating the environment for the awareness of the Global G.R.I.T. System™ and educating others to understand that grit can be developed and there is now a process and system in which to do so.

What does putting yourself and others through the Global G.R.I.T. System™ ultimately do? It will improve productivity and performance. By having team members go through the Global G.R.I.T. System™ in an environment in which they choose the grit for each element, they learn. And learning, in the workplace, while providing development tools, builds confidence. This confidence builds the belief. This belief increases motivation, which in turn influences cognition, which alters the way we think (aka brain processes), and opens our mind up to be willing to adopt a growth mindset approach and apply the Global G.R.I.T. System™ to every setting we encounter. Team members will have a stronger understanding of the responsibilities of their job, providing the confidence that enhances their performance and creates the environment in which the other pillars of grit, that one may need to work on, can be developed. As Anthony Mirabile so eloquently states, "Confidence is contagious. The more confidence you build, the more your standard deviation from the mean is expanded, meaning you can achieve things you never thought were possible before."

So how do we create the awareness of the Global G.R.I.T. System™? Culture. The work culture you create influences the environment around your team, which impacts their ability and perception to process the information given to them. The storage, processing, and assimilation methods for information contribute to how new knowledge is learned.[16] Thus, culture plays a significant role in conditioning and reinforcement learning styles and explains why certain programs are less effective than others, and why many programs do not "stick" with your team members. It is also essential for you to be aware of the fact that various dimensions of learning styles build self-efficacy.[17] In other words, if a team member takes the grit type indicator assessment and their dominant grit type is a Trustworthy Titan, their learning of the other areas of the grit types in the Global G.R.I.T. System™ are going to be different from that of a Go-Getter.

Allowing the autonomy in which team members learn the techniques and tools of the Global G.R.I.T. System™ is going to prove essential for their success to enhance their performance in the other areas of grit. I talk further about this and the different learning styles, depending on the type of grit, in Chapter 10.

Having the framework of the Global G.R.I.T. System™, with the four pillars that make up the elements of grit, understanding the process behind the application of the Global G.R.I.T. System™, and learning the four different types of grit within the Global G.R.I.T. System™ creates a system for companies, individuals, teams, leaders, and many more to increase productivity, improve workplace culture, and enhance performance. It is the innovation needed to gain, train, and retain top talent and to realize that anyone can develop grit; they just need a system. It will reduce turnover, increase employee engagement, and create a culture of excellence while developing an organization full of people with grit who are ready for when grit chooses them.

Who is the Global G.R.I.T. System™ for?

The Global G.R.I.T. System™ holds universal value that can serve a wide range of individuals, organizations, leaders, teams, and communities, from all walks of life. Here's who stands to gain from adopting this groundbreaking system:

- **Entire Companies:** The Global G.R.I.T System™ is a blueprint for collective success. Implementing this system, organization-wide, transforms the corporate culture, aligning everyone from the C-suite to the front lines under the unifying principles of grit. It elevates operational efficiencies, enhances team cohesiveness, and creates a culture of excellence that drives both employee satisfaction and business performance.

- **Business Leaders and Executives:** In a competitive marketplace where the only constant is change, the ability to exhibit grit in all areas becomes a distinct competitive advantage. This system equips business leaders with the tools to instill grit and develop it within their organizational culture, making it part of their brand's DNA.

- **Team Members and Employees:** Those on the front lines of any operation can utilize the Global G.R.I.T System™ to hone their individual capabilities, encouraging a cohesive, resilient, and highly effective team environment.

- **Entrepreneurs:** In the high-stakes world of start-ups and small businesses, grit can make the difference between failure and success. Entrepreneurs will find the Global G.R.I.T. System™ invaluable for navigating the complexities and uncertainties inherent in starting and scaling a business.

- **Educational Institutions:** Professors, teachers, and students alike can benefit from the Global G.R.I.T. System™ framework, applying and developing its principles to both academic and life challenges, thereby nurturing the next generation of gritty individuals.

- **Veterans and Military Personnel:** The transition from military life to a civilian setting can be filled with hardships, challenges, and complex adjustments. The Global G.R.I.T. System™ provides actionable strategies and practical solutions for these dedicated individuals to adapt, thrive, and flourish in an unfamiliar environment.

- **Individuals Facing Personal Challenges:** Whether navigating major life shifts like unemployment or divorce, or confronting emotional hardships such as grief or PTSD, the Global G.R.I.T. System™ provides a robust psychological foundation for cultivating resilience and elevating all facets of grit.
- **Community Organizations:** From local charities to global nonprofits, organizations aimed at social betterment can harness the power of the Global G.R.I.T. System™ to elevate their mission and multiply their impact.
- **Parents and Caregivers:** The principles of the Global G.R.I.T. System™ are foundational life skills that can and should be instilled from an early age. Parents can use the Global G.R.I.T. System™ as a blueprint for raising children who are resilient, gritty, empathetic, and ready to face the challenges of the world.
- **Everyday Heroes:** The Global G.R.I.T. System™ can help anyone live a life of purpose, achieve personal goals, and rise above the setbacks that life invariably places in our path. It's a universal roadmap to a life well-lived.

The Global G.R.I.T. System™ is for anyone who aspires to transform challenges into stepping stones for growth, to become not just a survivor, but a thriver in the complicated, beautiful journey that is life.

"The Global G.R.I.T. System™ provides a vast degree of insight, knowledge, and transparency to leaders and their team to have a solid foundation to build development plans, growth plans, career plans, and can help identify if someone is better suited for a different role in the organization in which they can thrive. Society is extremely quick to write people

off; however, if they go through the Global
G.R.I.T. System™, it will allow the individual,
the team, and the leaders, to be placed in
the best position to succeed."

Anthony Mirabile
Managing Director, Asset and Wealth
Management Division, Goldman Sachs

10 Key Leadership Lessons From This Chapter:

- Leadership is not a skill. Leadership is a behavior.

- The four pillars of G.R.I.T. as the foundation to develop grit:

  1. Get it Done
  2. Reframe Thinking
  3. Impact Others
  4. Take Responsibility

- You will be dominant in one specific area of grit. The four types of grit in the Global G.R.I.T. System™:

  1. Go-Getter
  2. Reframer
  3. Innovator
  4. Trustworthy Titan

- Identify which grit type you are using the Grit Type Indicator™.

- If you wait for tomorrow, tomorrow will never come.

- Emotions can be used as a major advantage if we know how to use them correctly. By choosing the emotion before it chooses us we use cognition to control emotion, and we can control our thoughts with how we view situations.

- What creates the foundation for organizational innovation are the individuals within the organization.

- The decisions you make don't just affect you, it affects those around you. Choose wisely.

- Grit can be taught. The Global G.R.I.T. System™ addresses the myths of grit which creates a new belief surrounding grit. Changing the belief, changes the motivation in individuals and teams, which influences cognition and changes brain patterns to alter the way one thinks. Brain processes modify and adapt, leading to a growth mindset that aids in the application of the Global G.R.I.T. System™, demonstrating how grit can be developed in anyone.

- The framework, the process, and the types of grit make up the system of developing grit. The Global G.R.I.T. System™ cultivates a team of individuals who can learn and apply grit through confidence gained as a result of the process, leading to improved productivity and performance in individuals, teams, and as an organization as a whole.

CHAPTER 6

Get it Done:
The "G" in the Global G.R.I.T. System™

"The way to get started is to quit talking and begin doing."

Walt Disney

GET IT DONE: Why it's Part of the Grit Mentality

You may be familiar with the Eisenhower Matrix, which can assist individuals in categorizing tasks in order of their importance.[1] When looking at the diagram, which box do you find yourself in frequently?

Urgent & Important	Not Urgent & Important
1	2
3	4
Urgent & Not Important	Not Urgent & Not Important

Acting with urgency is part of the grit mentality. It is a key aspect of the growth mindset because it helps individuals seize opportunities, overcome challenges, and make progress toward their goals. It fosters a proactive and determined approach to learning and development.[2] Think about this. Your phone rings, or you receive a text message and you feel an urge to immediately text back or pick up the phone. Perhaps you receive an email or text message from your favorite clothing store, and they pull you in with their "last chance–today only–30% off," and you click on the link. Before you know it, you are buying that new suit jacket that you probably didn't need. Why? Because you were tempted by urgency. I know, I've been there!

When faced with a time limit we often experience a heightened sense of focus that compels us to prioritize completing a specific task by a certain deadline through fear of missing out.[3] As such, urgent tasks become prioritized even though important tasks may have greater outcomes.[4] This is where the go-getter excels. They are able to complete urgent tasks quickly, but they tend to stay in the important and not urgent box of the Eisenhower Matrix, as they complete the necessary tasks before they become urgent. They focus on what's important and are task oriented with a process they follow, as important tasks are often more challenging than others, but being competitive, they like to tackle those first. If something needs to get done, they will just do it then and there, versus waiting for another time, because if they wait, they have become the "hunted" and lose their position as the hunter. A go-getter will never let that happen. If we refer back to the Eisenhower Matrix, the "important and urgent" box requires "doing." Go-getters will have that complete before the rest of the grit types have finished their breakfast that morning. That's how they operate. Fast-paced, get it done, because they want to focus on the important tasks that are not urgent to avoid having to be in the urgent box. They are task-oriented so they like to schedule and organize their time.

Go-getters thrive in box two in the Eisenhower Matrix, which is the important and not urgent box. If something creeps in that does become urgent, they will want it off their agenda as quickly as possible as they will see it as an annoyance because it prevents them from being able to schedule and manage their time effectively. If a task is urgent but not important, they won't even consider it, they will delegate it.[5] They will delegate it to someone else who will find that task important to them. However, if a task is not important and not urgent, the go-getter will delete that task altogether. It is unnecessary, a waste of time, and they don't see value in it. Go-getters value their time impeccably, and do not give it away to meaningless tasks that either a) somebody else who finds it important can do or b) have no value to what they are trying to achieve for the team or individually.

The go-getter is someone who is proactive, motivated, and takes initiative. They are incredibly driven and determined and have the "never give up" mentality. If you remember back to the process in the Global G.R.I.T. System™ in Chapter 5, what creates motivation for the go-getters? Why are they so motivated to just get on with the task at hand? Belief. They believe in themselves. Even if others don't. They aren't concerned with what others think, they focus on what they know they are capable of accomplishing. If they are unsure of what they are capable of they do it anyway, because they have the belief that they can. This motivates them to do it, which influences their cognition, which alters their brain patterns, and allows them to adopt a growth mindset.

Go-getters will take calculated risks, and research has shown this improves workplace outcomes.[6] They visualize success, increasing their confidence, which leads to belief, which leads to motivation. In this way they adopt the process in the Global G.R.I.T. System™ outlined in Chapter 5. They learn from setbacks and negative outcomes. They don't let it *defeat* them, they allow it to *inform* them. Inform them of what they can do better next time. They view challenges as opportunities to do better next time. They never give up. They refine their approach, which increases their chance of success in the future. They are the hunters. They are the ones who pursue something relentlessly, are proactive, and are consistently seeking opportunities and knowledge.[7]

How Do We Enhance Our "G" in the Global G.R.I.T. System™?

To get things done, you need confidence. Because what does confidence do? It creates belief. The belief creates the motivation. The motivation influences our cognition, and influencing our cognition alters our brain processes, and altering our brain processes allows us to adopt the growth mindset. By adopting the growth mindset, this allows the application of the G in the Global G.R.I.T. System™. As Anthony Mirabile of Goldman Sachs says, "Confidence is contagious." So too is fear and self-doubt, if the environment allows it. When you create an environment of learning for not just you, but for your team, then everyone will learn and grow. Fear spreads like rot. Confidence spreads with growth. Choose your catalyst for change.

So How Do We Create Confidence?

- **Write down your strengths.** Identify what you are really good at. Your passions. Your skills. Ask yourself, what makes YOU unique? Why are you valuable to your team? Ask yourself, why do you do what you do? What's your "why"?
- **Actively learn new skills.** When we expand our knowledge, it prepares us.[8] It prepares us for what's to come. When a situation

unfolds, we have answers that others may not, and thus our confidence increases as a leader to be able to help others when they need it most. Attending training workshops, seminars, leadership programs, or seeking out a coach or mentor are incredible ways to learn new skills and identify new passions.

- **Identify habits.** It is essential to identify your habits in order to eradicate the bad and amplify the good. We need good habits to carry out the tasks that need to be completed in order to attain goals. It is a process. When you realize the good habits you can harness and nurture, your confidence surrounding the tasks will increase.

- **Build your "culture of excellence."** Having excellence around you provides a strong support system so you receive feedback that you can learn from. It will keep you accountable, and in turn you will receive encouragement which will build your confidence and subsequently your belief.

- **Celebrate your achievements.** Remember what I said earlier about fear spreading like rot? Well so too does negativity. Instead of focusing on what you can't do, focus on what you can. Instead of focusing on your weaknesses, celebrate your successes and build on your strengths.

Having a "Get it Done" Attitude Versus Feeling Overwhelmed

Shifting from feeling overwhelmed and starting or stopping halfway to a "get it done" attitude can be achieved by understanding why you feel overwhelmed. Take a look at the number of responsibilities you have taken on, highlight your time management, address who your support network is, and assess your "culture of excellence."

Ways to Overcome This Feeling of Being Overwhelmed:

- **Set boundaries**
- **Prioritize tasks** (remember the Eisenhower Matrix)
- **Schedule your time** wisely, including small breaks throughout the day to refresh with water, food, sunlight (remember the five pillars discussed in Chapter 3).

- **Time blocking** to optimize productivity, with no distractions. Be disciplined with your time blocking and don't allow anything else to disrupt that time you have blocked in order to complete important tasks so they do not become urgent.

- **Delegate.** Oftentimes, we can take on too much. Use your culture of excellence around you. Who can you enlist to help you? A team member? A friend? A work colleague? A coach? A mentor? Use their expertise and their help; they have strengths in areas where you may be weak.

- **Say no more often.** You can't please everyone. It is perfectly okay to say no. If you try to please everyone, you will end up pleasing no one, so understand that it is okay to say no if it does not align with your goals, values, or purpose.

By implementing these strategies you'll be able to shift from feeling overwhelmed to adopting a "get it done" attitude and increase your productivity and success. Remember, hard times don't last forever. In the moment of carrying out a difficult task or something you know has to get done, don't give up, don't put it off, just get it done, because it won't last forever. Once it is done, it is done, and you can focus on the next task at hand.

Why We Need the "G" in the Global G.R.I.T. System™

When we get things done it demonstrates commitment, not just for ourselves, but for others. When we take action to achieve what we set out to accomplish, we establish our need and dedication to our vision. This in turn builds momentum and fosters a growth mindset. Go-getters use challenges as opportunities for growth and they learn from mistakes, setbacks, failures, and apply that newfound knowledge into practice to open themselves up to new possibilities that may be greater than they were before the setbacks. When we take action and just "get it done," we develop the belief in our ability to achieve our goals and promote self-efficacy.[9] This then fuels further action over and over. Stronger leadership abilities are gained when one takes action, and lends to skills such as being practical, assertive, and getting to the point. Go-getters don't like to waste time and move at a very fast pace. If they see a threat in their way, they will want to remove it immediately, particularly if it poses a threat to their team. They have the "hunter" mentality. They make decisions quickly, they dislike inaction, and they solve problems quickly.

Why Do Some of Us Struggle With the "G" in the Global G.R.I.T. System™?

Taking action involves the risk of failure, which to some may be intimidating. This fear of failure can spread into other areas of life, slowing down the progress of the "G." Remember, fear spreads like rot. Having a lack of confidence in our abilities means a lack of self-belief, which decreases motivation. It can be difficult to take action without confidence. If you find you have team members that lack this ability, one way to counteract it is to provide an environment in which they have the autonomy to learn in the style that suits them, whether it be auditory, visual, or practical. In doing so, you build confidence, which leads to the motivation needed to progress in this area. Some may become overwhelmed by the decisions that need to be made when carrying out the "G" in the Global G.R.I.T. System™, especially at such a fast pace. Breaking down the complexity of a situation and dealing with one thing at a time helps with this. Using the Eisenhower Matrix to prioritize tasks helps enormously. It also helps to minimize distractions and use time blocking. If that means changing the environment in order to complete tasks, then so be it. Taking ourselves out of our comfort zone and familiar surroundings allows for greater focus on the task at hand. Perfectionism is also an issue when it comes to utilizing the "G" in the Global G.R.I.T. System™. This can hinder the ability to "get things done," because perfectionists will become hyper-focused on ensuring everything is right, rather than complete, often meaning they won't finish a task or take far longer to finish. While perfectionists' pursuit of excellence is admirable, their self-imposed standards of perfection hinders progress. This can lead to burnout and limit their ability to adapt and innovate. Think of the lioness in the Serengeti. If the lioness waited for perfection, her pride would die of starvation. Perfectionism also hinders progress with development.[10] It doesn't allow for failures, and yet this is where the majority of growth occurs, in our setbacks.

A few of the strategies that help with perfectionism include building self-awareness in one's behavior, thoughts, and emotions. It also helps to understand the costs and benefits associated with perfectionism and how it holds people back from their potential. Many times people have limiting beliefs around perfectionism that are often caused by deep-seated beliefs about what success really looks like, and that their worth is tied to how "perfect" everything needs to be. One of the keys to shifting from perfectionism to a "get it done" attitude is to set realistic goals, identify the tasks that need to be carried out to achieve those goals, and then highlight the good habits that need to be fostered in order to carry out the tasks. This helps switch the focus to *progress* rather than *perfection*. Not being perfect on a task means to take a risk for a perfectionist. Risks have been shown to be positive in a work environment, even if the outcome of that risk is failure.[11] Thus encouragement in this area is vital as it allows practicing trial and error and receiving feedback in order to change brain patterns out of a *perfectionist* mindset and into a *progress* mindset. This will help perfectionists adapt to a fast-paced environment, harnessing more of the "G" in the Global G.R.I.T. System™.

If You Are the "G" in the Global G.R.I.T. System™

If your grit type indicator assessment shows your dominance as a go-getter, this means you are in the driver's seat within your team. You typically prefer to be left alone to work and are fiercely independent with a strong-will to 'get things done'. You prefer to be in control and prefer freedom over your choices to lead your path. You don't have a lot of patience, and don't like to wait to get things done, propelling you to want immediate results. Decisiveness is your hallmark, whether it's in setting goals or addressing challenges head-on. Your competitive nature isn't just about winning; it's about achieving excellence and doing so with confidence. You have incredible laser-focus, which drives the intensity to achieve greatness. You have strong authority and are exemplary at problem-solving. Being the "G" in the Global G.R.I.T. System™ means inaction isn't just undesirable; it's intolerable. When given the freedom to lead, you excel. You work remarkably independently and are consistently aiming for the highest levels of success. Harnessing the "G" in the Global G.R.I.T. System™ isn't just a strategy, it's essential in leadership, as a team member and outside of the workplace. It will anchor you, creating a foundation of strength and purpose, even amidst storms. Use this element of your grit to navigate and persevere through adversity, by swiftly finding solutions, taking the authority, acting quickly to get things done and transforming the outcome. It's important to understand and recognize when to utilize other areas of your grit within the Global G.R.I.T. System™. There are moments when leaning heavily on the "G" in your grit might not be the most beneficial during specific adversities. For instance, during profound challenges, like the heart-wrenching loss of my son. A balanced approach to grit becomes pivotal, leading your team to understand all elements of the Global G.R.I.T. System™ and how they tie into one another, developing all four pillars.

Learning Points From the "G" in the Global G.R.I.T. System™

Remember, the go-getters don't wait for success to come to them. They take the initiative, set goals, and work tirelessly to achieve them. They hunt, they fail, they get back up, they learn, they apply, they pull from the strength of others. Remember the example I provided in Chapter 2? When I worked hard for many months to take the standard but failed the first time I didn't let it defeat me. I pulled from the strengths of others to help me in the areas I was weak and I got it done. Twelve weeks and five days later, after I failed it, I passed. Three hundred and forty one total days to pass the standard. Create deadlines for tasks that are hard to start and focus on what *actually* matters, instead of focusing on what you *think* matters. How do you differentiate between the two? Look at it objectively and seek external input from coaches or mentors if necessary to gain a clearer understanding. This will help mitigate the influence of confirmation bias (favoring information that confirms our existing belief), availability bias (relying on information that is readily available), and anchoring bias (being influenced by initial information).

Get it done. And celebrate your accomplishments along the way to your goals. If you wait, you are only delaying the inevitable and then it ultimately becomes urgent. The Eisenhower Matrix box you want to be in, and stay in, is important and not urgent. So get it done, and carry out the tasks today that will shape your future tomorrow.

"If you want something, go get it. Period."

Chris Gardner

10 Key Leadership Lessons From This Chapter:

- Hard times don't last forever.

- It's okay to say no.

- Be in the important and not urgent box, consistently.

- "Get it Done" means to be proactive, motivated, and take initiative.

- Confidence enhances the "G" in the Global G.R.I.T. System™ and the environment in which to learn that confidence is crucial.

- Delegate the tasks that are not important but urgent.

- Delete the tasks that are not important and not urgent.

- The "G" in the Global G.R.I.T. System™ is important as it demonstrates commitment, not just for ourselves, but for others.

- To harness the power of the "G" in the Global G.R.I.T. System™, switch the focus to *progress* rather than *perfection* and encourage others to do the same. This will change their brain patterns out of a perfectionist mindset and into a *progress* mindset.

- The go-getters hunt, they fail, they get back up, they learn, they apply, and they pull from the strength of others.

CHAPTER 7

Reframe Thinking:
The "R" in the Global G.R.I.T. System™

"Be in control of your thoughts and you'll be in control of your life."

Lara Jones

REFRAME THINKING: Why it's Part of the Grit Mentality

Aaron Beck, the psychiatrist who developed cognitive therapy, said that our cognition is influenced by automatic thoughts, cognitive distortions, and underlying beliefs.[1] As human beings, we are wired to think negatively, causing cognitive distortions in many cases.[2] Research shows we have around six thousand thoughts a day, and out of that number, around eighty percent of our thoughts are negative.[3] Approximately ninety percent of our thoughts are repetitive, meaning that on a daily basis we have more negative thoughts than positive ones. This means we are highly influenced by our negative thoughts because of the repetition. Emotional disorders, such as anxiety and depression, are linked to repetitive negative thinking (RNT). Our perception of situations plays an important role in the development and maintenance of our emotions.[4] Think of it like this: the brain is Velcro for negative experiences and Teflon for positive ones. Meaning, our unconscious memory—also known as our "implicit memory"—which is our underlying expectations, beliefs, and mood, is pushed into a negative direction automatically.[5]

In the late 1950's Albert Ellis developed the rational-emotive therapy (RET), and Aaron Beck developed cognitive therapy (CT). However, RET can be traced back to the work of Marcus Aurelius and Epictetus' Enchiridion, who believed individuals are disturbed by the way they view events around them versus the events themselves.[6] Human beings are often trapped in the irrational "shoulds" and "musts," leading to negative thinking.[7] This in turn leads to negative emotions and thus negative behavioral patterns which results in distorted beliefs about situations.[8] Subsequently, reframing thoughts in any given situation will lead to a positive change of the distorted beliefs and thus lead to positive emotional and behavioral patterns.[9] Cognitive restructuring (reframing of thoughts) is the most effective treatment for Post Traumatic Stress Disorder (PTSD) by identifying the "cues" to the traumatic event and altering the perception of the stimulus.[10] Intrusive memories that are being triggered by cues, are the re-experiencing of an event that is not happening in the present but a memory of the past[11] and thus through the reframing of our thinking, we are able to alter our approach to a given situation.

David D. Burns MD, a professor emeritus in the Department of Psychiatry and Behavioral Sciences at the Stanford University School of Medicine, conducted research on the influence of distorted thinking. His work, largely built on Beck's research, identified ten cognitive distortions commonly observed during negative emotional experiences.[12]

Cognitive Disorder | *Definition*

- **All or nothing thinking** | *One mistake makes you feel like a complete failure*
- **Overgeneralization** | *A negative event is viewed as a never-ending pattern*
- **Mental filter** | *Intense focus on the negatives while ignoring the positives*
- **Discounting the positives** | *You feel as though your accomplishments "do not count"*
- **Jumping to conclusions** | *Expecting things will turn out badly without evidence*
- **Magnification or minimization** | *Blowing things out of proportion or shrinking a moment's importance*
- **Emotional reasoning** | *Believing that your emotional reaction makes something true even if the evidence proves otherwise*
- **"Should" statements** | *Criticizing yourself or other people by stating what you "should have done"*
- **Labeling** | *Identifying with your shortcomings; you call yourself a "fool" or "loser" for making an error*
- **Personalization or blame** | *Blaming yourself for something you weren't responsible for or blaming other people and overlooking your own contributions to the problem*

An explanation as to why the majority of our thoughts on a daily basis are negative[13] can be linked to our survival instinct and evolution. Ten thousand years ago if you heard a rustling in the bushes it was most likely a predator. Thus, our thinking automatically went into survival mode and our brains immediately thought the worst as a means of protecting us and to keep us safe.[14]

Throughout our evolution our species has developed strategies for survival, including creating separations and forming boundaries between one mental state and another, keeping physical and mental systems in a healthy balance through maintaining stability for a healthy balance, and approaching opportunities while avoiding threats. Our constantly changing conditions, in any environment, consistently disturb these systems, resulting in "suffering". As such, pain and distress are evolved through neural networks, making us aware when separations have subsided, stability is uncertain, disappointment with opportunities occur, and when threats are apparent.[15] This makes it difficult when adversity hits or a situation occurs in which only the negative can be perceived in that given moment. However, the key word to focus on here is "evolved." Our neural networks are not permanent. We have the power to change them.

Reframers are typically steady and methodical in their approach, owing to their process-driven minds. They have excellent problem solving skills and have a need for structure and organization, which is why they are brilliant at being able to reframe their thoughts in an orderly manner. Reframers are typically quiet and introverted because they focus on their thoughts and they like to have the facts and data.

Steven Trujillo, friend and Managing Partner of Northwestern Mutual, which is an American financial services mutual organization and Fortune 100 company, describes the reframing of thoughts perfectly. He told the story of when he transitioned from law enforcement, where he carried out two years of street patrol, then went into investigations for four years, undercover narcotics for two, and was promoted to sergeant for almost two years. All in all, nearly ten years of service. In October of 2008 Steve decided to leave law enforcement and joined the Northwestern Mutual December training class, officially starting his business with Northwestern in January of 2009. This was during the Great Recession. The first quarter of 2009 was recorded as the worst time of the recession, with the market bottoming in March of 2009. Many of Steve's friends questioned his decision to leave law enforcement for an industry he didn't know anything about at the time. However, he said, "All I could think about was the opportunity." Steve had started out with high hopes and his dream that he was meant for something more in his life. However, shortly into his new career, he faced immense rejection like nothing he had felt before. "It paralyzed me," he said. In March of 2009 his marriage broke up and he found himself living in a very small apartment. He got divorced later that year. Steve faced immense stress coupled with financial uncertainty. A perfect combination to start thoughts spiraling into what could have resulted into depression and failure. Steve recalls going home in the middle of the day, sitting down in his recliner, putting his head back, tears streaming down his face. He cried himself to sleep. Then he remembers waking up and looking himself in the mirror and giving himself a pep talk. He said, "I knew I couldn't change my past, but I can choose a better future." Later that year, in 2009, he finished in the top ten in the entire company in Northwestern's Bronze category.

So how did he do it? "I was constantly having to reframe my negative thoughts," he said, saying he believes "We have to truly guard our minds to be intentional with reframing every negative thought because it is overwhelming, but naturally we are programmed that way." He said there was a famous quote he lived by, by Mike Todd, an American theater and film producer, who said, "Being broke is temporary, being poor is a state of mind."

Ben Carson, a retired neurosurgeon, academic, author, and politician who grew up in poverty said, "People with the 'right mindset' can have everything taken away from them, and they'll pull themselves up. You take somebody with the wrong mindset, you can give them everything in the world and they'll work their way right back down to the bottom".[16] Simply put, brains wire themselves to their surroundings. This is essential to understand how our own perception of situations and surroundings contribute to the development of thoughts in our children. The "state of mind" we adopt most likely will be the "state of mind" our children will develop, owing to early attachment experiences contributing to later functioning, including our neurobiology and culture.[17]

Jason France, who I introduced in earlier chapters, is the co-founder of Suffer City, and a former Marine Raider. He is also a certified neuro linguistic programmer (NLP). He says that Noam Chomsky, an American theoretical linguist, describes language as a mathematical product with sentences as mathematical foundations of syntactic structures. "Language is a key to unlocking the minds of yourself and others," Jason told me. In other words, communication is an essential aspect of human existence. Chomsky's theory of language acquisition identified that we exercise written and oral communication by storing information in our brain, unconsciously, and we use neural circuits in the brain to contain linguistic signals.[18] The words we use and the way we say them affects our emotional reaction to a situation, owing to the connection we have with particular words that we create every day. One word change in a sentence can completely change the architecture and thus the meaning. Therefore, if we change the words we use toward a situation from negative to positive, new neural networks will develop and alter the brain patterns that automatically fire off the signals to determine which emotion to exhibit, and this affects our behaviors and actions.

How Do We Enhance Our "R" in the Global G.R.I.T. System™?

Good things happen all the time around us, but because we are hardwired to always look for the threats, we often miss or overlook the good. We don't actively look for positive news, which is why social media has been found to be addicting to many, because it focuses on negativity and as human beings, we are hard wired with the negativity bias.[19] We have to work hard to become aware of the positive facts around us, and turn them into positive experiences.[20] Neurons in our brain become more responsive to input depending how active they are, and they receive more oxygen through increased blood flow.[21] When focusing on the negative we may feel that one thing after another can sometimes go wrong, because our neurons associated with the negative facts and situations are heightened. As we allow our focus to be on the negative, more blood flows to that region of the brain. If we flipped that and focused on the positive when a negative happened, so too can the reverse effect take place. The blood flow will go to different neurons looking for the positive in a negative situation, causing them to be more responsive when a negative situation occurs, but the neural network is now hardwired to see the positive.[22] When neurons fire together, they wire together through strengthening their synapses to form new ones, forming new neural networks, which is how we learn and create memories.[23] Research has found that positive feelings increase resilience and counteract the effects of negative experiences.[24]

Paul Richardson, SVP for three major divisions of Milwaukee Tools, a Fortune 500 company, shared his insights into grit and the type of grit he had to pull from when a personal tragedy unfolded in his life at the tender age of eighteen. Paul's twin brother was stabbed to death right next to him, with Paul being a victim of the crime also, but surviving. Only three months earlier his best friend had been shot and murdered right next to Paul. Paul had an incredibly tough time for two to three years following the loss of his best friend and brother, with self-destructive behavior and living with survivor's guilt. He didn't think he deserved to be successful or happy. What eventually got him out of this downward negative spiral were the words his mother said to him one day that reframed his thinking. She made it clear to Paul how his brother does not get the opportunities that he does and told him his brother would not be proud of his actions. She went on to say that if Paul was not going to make the most of his opportunities in life, he was being disrespectful to his brother, who no longer had that opportunity. Paul stated that after having that conversation he had a paradigm shift, and from that day forward he wanted to be the best he possibly could be in anything he did, whether it be as a father, a husband, an athlete, a leader, or business professional. It takes grit to do that every single day.

It is important to note that reframers typically view experiences as subjective, meaning they use their individual experiences, thoughts, and perceptions to influence their reality. This is why they excel in this area of grit. Reframing situations, thoughts, and experiences comes naturally to them even if they have not experienced severe negative situations.

Techniques That Help Develop the "R" in the Global G.R.I.T. System™

Once you identify positive facts about situations, the work begins when you turn the positive *facts* into positive *experiences*.[25] The techniques listed can assist in reframing thoughts, perspectives, transforming situations, and lead to a more positive and constructive outlook when faced challenging situations in the future.

- **Visualization.** Envision your future self succeeding. Picture yourself achieving your goals, with every detail vivid, feeling the emotions and sensations of that success.

- **Positive self-talk.** Replace negative thoughts with empowering statements. Whenever a doubt creeps in, tell yourself, "I am capable, I've overcome challenges before, and I can do it again."

- **Positive affirmations.** Repeat daily: "I am resilient, I trust in my abilities, and every day I grow stronger and more confident in my journey."

- **Challenge your assumptions and biases.** Ask yourself: "What if I'm wrong?" or "How else can I see this situation?" Consider alternative possibilities.

- **Look for the lesson.** Ask yourself: "What's the opportunity in this challenge?"

- **Practice gratitude.** Appreciate what you have and what you've achieved. Ask yourself: "What am I proud of?" or "Who or what am I grateful for?"

- **Shift your attention.** Focus on what you are grateful for in the situation to encourage an alternative perspective

- **Seek input from others.** Be open to constructive criticism and different perspectives. Ask yourself: "What can I learn from others?" or "Who can help me see this differently?"

- **Language reframing.** Use positive and empowering language to reframe negative or limiting thoughts. This can influence our beliefs, attitudes, and behaviors, leading to a more positive and productive mindset overall.

- **Finding opportunities.** Look for the potential benefits or opportunities that may arise from the situation.

- **Mindfulness.** Practice being present and observe your thoughts and emotions without judgment, allowing for a fresh perspective.

- **Humor and playfulness** *(depending on the level of severity of the circumstance).* Inject humor or playfulness into the situation to encourage a different perspective.

- **Perspective shift.** Look at the situation from a different point of view or consider how someone else might perceive it.

Remember, reframing thinking is not about denying reality or ignoring problems, but about choosing to focus on what you can control and influence, and finding ways to turn adversity into an advantage. It takes practice and patience, but the payoff is worth it. You will achieve a more resilient, adaptable, and positive mindset that can help you overcome challenges, not just for yourself, but for your team and those around you. This will help you achieve your goals.

The broaden-and-build theory explains the characteristics and purpose of certain positive emotions, such as joy, interest, contentment, and love.[26] The theory suggests that positive emotions expand people's immediate range of thoughts and actions, leading to the development of long-lasting innovative solutions, including physical, intellectual, social, and psychological resources.

Let's look at a simple task. Change one word in a sentence and see how it changes everything. For example, "look what happened to me" can be changed to, "look what *revealed* me" or "look what happened *for* me." It changes physically how you feel about the statement and thus outlook on the situation. I personally prefer to use the word "revealed" in this sentence, because it implies that something new has unfolded and causes the individual to view his or her actions, versus potentially having a tougher time around the concept of "for me." To give an example, when I discussed my son's passing in Chapter 2, I don't like to think of his passing as something that happened for me, because the pain surrounding his death is so great. If I wanted something to happen for me, it would have been to let him live. Thus, when I use the word "revealed," it peels back a layer and forces me to look at myself in the mirror and say, "Look who you are now because your son passed away. Look what fire has emerged through using trauma and grief as your fuel versus letting it consume and burn you." There are circumstances when you can use the word "for" in that sentence, such as a job loss. However, it is up to you to witness the feelings that emerge as a result of changing one word in the sentence and seeing which one results in a more positive light. As Carl Jung said, "Two people see the same object, but they never see it in such a way that the images they receive are absolutely identical."[27] The same can be said of feelings. How one changes one word could exhibit slightly different feelings than that of another, owing to their connotation, understanding, and beliefs associated with that word.

Reframers are adaptable because they pull from their "R" in the Global G.R.I.T. System™ and they know when to use certain elements of the grit for certain situations. As an example, when you learned of my tragedy and trauma in Chapter 2, you may have asked, "How did she get through that?" I pulled from the "R" in my grit at that moment, and reframed how I thought about the situation. If I didn't, it could have killed me.

A Shift in Perspective

If there has been a major event that has taken place that completely altered your path in life, where did your thoughts just go? Did you see it as a negative event or a positive event? In many cases, it will have led to a negative event. Now think of how that event has affected your ability to make decisions.

Think of a negative situation in your life that has taken place and how it has altered your motivation to do something. Upon thinking of the negative situation, how did that event influence your decision making? What physical feeling did you feel in your body when you recalled the negative event? What emotions are you experiencing when recalling that negative event? Write them down:

- Describe a negative situation. (Example: Look what happened to me, my son died.) _____

  _____

- Describe the physical feeling. _____

  _____

- What emotions are you experiencing right now as you think about the situation? _____

  _____

- How did it influence your decision-making? _____

  _____

- Now change one or more words / add words from the sentence you wrote to describe your situation to create a positive connotation. (Example: Look what *revealed* me, *when* my son died.) _____

  _____

- Describe how this may have altered your decision-making when you read the description of the reframed situation. _____

  _____

- Describe the physical feeling attached to the situation now that you have reframed the sentence. _____

  _____

- What emotions are you feeling about the reframed situation? _____

  _____

Practice Reframing:

- **Thought awareness:** Develop awareness of your thoughts and actively challenge negative or unhelpful language patterns.
- **Catch and replace:** Pay attention to negative or limiting thoughts and consciously replace them with more positive and empowering language. Original thought: "I can't do this. It's too difficult." Reframed thought: "This may be challenging, but I am capable of learning and growing through the process."

  In this example, the original thought is negative and self-limiting. Through reframing, the thought is transformed into a positive and empowering statement. It encourages a mindset of possibility through acknowledging the challenge while emphasizing personal growth and capability.

- **Positive affirmations:** Use affirmations to reinforce positive beliefs and thoughts about yourself and the situation. This in turn will build confidence. Confidence will build the belief. What does the belief do? Creates motivation. What does the motivation do? It influences cognition, which alters the brain processes, which allows one to develop a growth mindset that can adopt the affirmations to becoming automatic.

- **Cognitive restructuring:** Identify and reframe cognitive distortions or irrational beliefs by replacing them with more rational and realistic thoughts.
- **Journaling:** Write down your thoughts and reframe them on paper, allowing for reflection and the opportunity to reframe with intention.
- **Surround yourself with positive language:** Surround yourself with positive influences, such as uplifting books, podcasts, coaches, mentors, or affirmations to reinforce positive language patterns.
- **Practice self-compassion:** Be patient and kind to yourself during this process. It takes time to change ingrained language habits.

Consistency and practice are key. Over time, you can develop a habit of using more positive and empowering language, which can positively impact your mindset and overall well-being, which also impacts those around you, including your team. This will have a significant impact on personal growth, well-being, and overall quality of life. By consistently practicing these techniques, you can gradually shift your language patterns and cultivate a more positive and empowering mindset. Through the practice of reframing, it can bring several benefits, including:

- **Positive mindset:** It helps cultivate a more positive and optimistic outlook on any situation that may occur.
- **Stress reduction:** It can reduce stress by shifting your focus from the negative to positive aspects of a situation.
- **Improved problem-solving:** It encourages a more creative and solution-oriented approach to challenges.
- **Enhanced resilience:** It builds resilience by promoting a mindset of growth and learning.
- **Superior communication:** It enhances communication skills by using constructive and empowering language.
- **Increased self-confidence:** It boosts self-confidence and self-belief by reframing self-limiting thoughts.
- **Emotional well-being:** It contributes to emotional well-being by promoting positive emotions and reducing negativity.

- **Better relationships:** It fosters more productive and positive relationships by promoting empathy, understanding, and positive interactions.

Why We Need The "R" in the Global G.R.I.T. System™

Have you ever found yourself stuck in a negative mindset, focusing on the challenges ahead instead of looking for the opportunities and solutions in the moment? While it's natural to feel discouraged and overwhelmed at times, adopting a fixed, defeatist attitude will hold you back from achieving your goals. That's where reframing thinking comes in. Reframing means looking at a situation from a different angle, shifting your focus from what's wrong to what's right, and finding a more empowering narrative. Instead of seeing setbacks as failures, you can see them as learning experiences and opportunities to grow. Instead of seeing others as threats or competitors, you can see them as potential collaborators or mentors. Instead of seeing yourself as a victim or a burden, you can see yourself as a resilient and resourceful person who can overcome challenges and make a difference.

Reframing thinking is not just a cognitive trick or a mindset hack, but an integral part of the grit mentality. Grit requires not only resilience and tenacity, but also optimism and adaptability. When you reframe your thinking, you not only increase your motivation and confidence, but also expand your creativity and problem-solving skills. You start to see possibilities where you used to see limitations, and you start to take action toward your vision instead of getting stuck in analysis paralysis or negative self-talk. The "R" in the Global G.R.I.T. System™ brings fresh insights to what might appear to be complex problems.

Why Do Some of Us Struggle with the "R" in the Global G.R.I.T. System™?

Remember that eighty percent of our thoughts are negative[28] and ninety percent are repetitive.[29] We have a lot going against us with the number of times negative thoughts play in our head. However, through the rewiring of the brain to create new neural networks we can absolutely change that and drown out the noise of the negative and pay more attention to the positive by reducing our negative thoughts. I mentioned earlier that when neurons receive more oxygen through increased blood flow as a result of them being more active, they become more responsive.[30] So we have to learn how to turn down the volume of the negative thoughts and increase the volume of the positive thoughts. This will also teach our brains over time how to reframe situations, so that it becomes automatic.

Confirmation bias[31] is one of the reasons why some of us may struggle to reframe our thinking. This is when we favor information that confirms existing beliefs instead of challenging those beliefs to see if there's a different answer that may prevail. In a team setting, it is critical that we don't just agree with each other, but rather keep each other accountable for those thoughts and challenge those beliefs in a productive and positive setting. We also face negativity bias.[32] If you don't know how to reframe your thoughts or do not practice it through a variety of techniques you will tend to give more weight to negative experiences and catastrophize the potential negative outcomes of a situation. These biases can influence how people perceive and interpret events, which also leads to a negative and fixed mindset.

Lack of awareness is another reason many may struggle with reframing. They may not be aware that it is even possible to train your brain and control the negativity bias for sustainable and long-term effects. Emotional attachment is another area that is difficult for some; they may not be able to let go of their negative thoughts or beliefs owing to an emotional attachment to that thinking. When my son passed away and I nearly lost my life, I didn't want to look for positives in a dire situation. So I didn't. But what I did do is look at it from my son's perspective and I changed one word in a sentence that I used to repeat over to myself. This changed my life. I pulled from the "R" in my grit and I stopped saying, "This happened to me" and instead said, "This revealed me." As a result it shifted my perspective, my negative thought patterns, and allowed my blood to flow to the areas of the brain that had the positive thoughts, creating new neural networks and altering my brain patterns.

Like anything, it takes time and it takes practice. If we don't practice, our mind can wander back to our original thoughts. In fact, mind-wandering has been linked to crucial parts of our daily lives, including learning and job productivity and happens constantly unless you are aware of it and control your thoughts. What is even more intriguing is that our wandering thoughts are the most limited in the morning, increase throughout the morning, and reach peak freedom of movement by midday.[33] They then start to tail off in the afternoon but increase again in the evening. This has ramifications for not just the workplace but education as well, suggesting that schedules that align with these daily patterns could improve efficiency. Thus, making important decisions and carrying out tasks that require structure with sustained attention are best carried out in the morning. Tasks that require more freedom of movement with thoughts, like brainstorming, are best to be carried out around midday or again in the evening. This is why oftentimes we end up putting off tasks that we otherwise would have completed if we had changed the order.

In education, classes that require creativity, such as art or music, are best taken around midday. In the workplace, if you need to have a brainstorming session, schedule it around late morning leading into midday. Understanding the times of the day that individuals within teams are most likely to go *off*-task and be the most focused *for* tasks is critical to increase productivity and team morale, leading to increased motivation.[34] You will also find that if you are the "R" in the Global G.R.I.T. System™ you will be the most productive in the morning and again in the afternoon. Paying attention to how we structure our days, based on the research just presented, is essential for developing the "R" in our grit.

If You Are the "R" in the Global G.R.I.T. System™

If your grit type indicator assessment shows your dominance as a reframer, this means you can quickly recognize problems others don't see. You can use this element of your grit to persevere through adversity by making the right decision when time allows you to do so while staying committed to that decision and creating structure where needed in order for others to be able to count on you. During times of adversity you will be able to devise a comprehensive navigation plan. You are also more likely to predict when adversity may hit while devising a plan to help minimize or prevent it from hitting hard not just for you, but for your team and for the organization. It is also important to recognize when you need to pull from other areas of your grit. Such as the G, I, and the T. This creates equity in your grit and leads your team to understand all elements of the Global G.R.I.T. System™ and how they tie in to one another, developing all four pillars.

Learning Points From the "R" in the Global G.R.I.T. System™

Remember, the "reframers" want to understand how we got to where we are and take on projects that others see as unsalvageable. They hunt, and by being thorough and careful they see patterns that emerge. They are the most productive when they are in control of the situation. The example I provided earlier in this chapter surrounding the most tragic event of my life is a prime example of how I pulled from the "R" in the Global G.R.I.T. System™ and reframed my thoughts around the situation. I took control of my thoughts and it altered my brain patterns over time. I celebrate my son for coming into my life, albeit physically for a brief time, rather than being distraught that he left. The emotions surrounding the distress did not serve me, my family, or others around me. When I reframed the situation to be about others, rather than me, it helped me to identify the feelings associated with the reframed situation, which in turn made my behavior and actions positive rather than destructive. How can you differentiate between the negative and positive and reframe your thinking on a consistent basis? Look at it objectively and seek external input from coaches or mentors to gain a clearer understanding. This will help mitigate the influence of confirmation bias (favoring information that confirms our existing belief), availability bias (relying on information that is readily available), and anchoring bias (being influenced by initial information).

Reframe your thinking. Let in new perspectives. If you stay in negative patterns with your thinking, you are only fueling the already burning fire, with more oxygen traveling to the neural network, in your brain, which causes it to burn stronger. The Eisenhower Matrix box you want to be in, and stay in, is box two, important and not urgent. Reframe your thinking of the tasks that may seem daunting and carry out the tasks today that will shape your future tomorrow.

"When we change the way we look at things, the things we look at change."

Wayne Dyer

10 Key Leadership Lessons From This Chapter:

- Reframers bring fresh insights to what may appear to be complex problems.

- Eighty percent of our thoughts are negative, ninety percent are repetitive.

- Reframers typically view experiences as subjective, meaning they use their individual experiences, thoughts, and perceptions to influence their reality.

- Turn the positive *facts* into positive *experiences*.

- Look at your situation from a different angle, shift your focus from what's wrong to what's right, and find a more empowering narrative for your situation.

- We are wired to have a negativity bias; we have to work hard and consistently to practice the concentration of positive thoughts to create new neural networks in our brain that will eventually become automatic.

- The time of day affects your learning ability and productivity for reframing situations. If you are an "R" in the Global G.R.I.T. System™ your most productive time to complete tasks are in the morning and early afternoon.

- When you reframe your thinking, you increase your confidence and belief. This will increase your motivation, which will influence your cognition and alter your brain processes to adopt a growth mindset and allow you to apply the reframing on a consistent basis and become sustainable. You will start to see possibilities where you used to see limitations.

- When neurons receive more oxygen through increased blood flow as a result of them being more active, they become more responsive. The more attention you give negative thoughts, the stronger they become. The more attention you give positive thoughts, the weaker the negative thoughts become. It takes time to build a new neural network, but practicing with the techniques and tools, daily, allows for reframing to become automatic.

- The reframers take on projects that others see as unsalvageable. They are thorough and careful, identify patterns that emerge, and are the most productive when they are in control of the situation.

CHAPTER 8

Impact Others:
The "I" in the Global
G.R.I.T. System™

"The meaning of life is to find your gift.
The purpose of life is to give it away."

Pablo Picasso

IMPACT OTHERS: Why it's Part of the Grit Mentality

A company's long-term viability is deeply reliant on its ability to innovate.[1] If you recall, in Chapter 5 I discussed what creates the foundation for organizational innovation. It is the employee's innovative behavior that has a positive influence on a company's innovation. So how do we harness the innovation from employees and our team? Through empowerment-focused leadership. Empowerment-focused leadership positively impacts the innovative behaviors of employees.[2] What do we mean by empowerment-focused leadership? It means to give autonomy to team members so they have the freedom to make choices about how they complete tasks, which in turn encourages self-reliance. It means providing your team members with the resources they need, the necessary tools and the training for them to be as effective as possible. Empowerment-focused leadership also means to offer support to others without micromanaging by offering guidance, feedback, and encouragement. It's the ability to enhance their skill sets, which in turn increases their confidence and allows team members to have a say in team level or project level decisions. This in turn increases their sense of ownership and accountability. What is the first part of the process when applying the Global G.R.I.T. System™ outlined in Chapter 5? Providing the environment to give autonomy to your team members. This creates belief. Now you have a team that is motivated to carry out innovative work because you provided them an environment in which they can do so and thrive.

Servant leadership and the way team members interact with one another are major driving forces that encourage innovation among employees.[3] Additionally, the way employees interact with one another, coupled with empowerment-focused leadership, is "significantly related to perceived insider status".[4] In other words, if the team members or employees feel that they are integral and valuable members of their organization, not through tenure or rank but by the emotional and psychological investment a team member feels toward their organization, then the innovation will increase. When a team member perceives themselves as an "insider" they feel a greater sense of belonging, ownership, and involvement in their workplace. The impact of this increases engagement, creates higher productivity, and leads to reduced turnover.[5] Thus, open communication and trust creates a catalyst for innovative ideas and problem-solving approaches.

To spark creativity, whether in a team or as an individual, ideas need to be fresh yet practical, with the ability to drive organizational growth. Creativity allows for both subtle, step-by-step improvements as well as groundbreaking shifts.[6] However, creativity is different from innovation in that creativity helps conceive new ideas, whereas innovation is the act of bringing these ideas to life. Because creativity often serves as the launching pad for innovation, it is incredibly important for leaders to be on the hunt for strategies that can nurture creativity. This, in turn, enhances the pathway for initiating innovative solutions.

It is critical that leaders impact others within their team and organization by demonstrating innovative behavior themselves.[7] This sets the example and creates an environment that advances growth and collaboration in teams, which is essential for the grit mentality. Leaders can impact others by providing mentorship, emotional support, and constructive feedback that inspires individual and collective growth and increases engagement. Aspiring leaders can learn positive leadership, which will influence the positive emotional experiences of others and improve the effectiveness of the overall organization.[8] To achieve the "I" in the Global G.R.I.I. System™ means to be motivated by something far more significant than personal gain. It requires a focus on creating positive change in others, which creates a significant impact, not just in your teams or within your organization, but in the lives of those around you, including your community. Leaders have the power to influence the culture of their organization and inspire their team to strive for greatness. In doing so, leaders who impact others positively through effective communication, support, and empowerment build a sense of trust and loyalty in their team. Furthermore, impacting others with inspiration creates belief and thus motivation, which influences cognition and alters brain patterns, allowing teams to work together toward shared goals. This will naturally drive productivity owing to this new culture of collaboration, innovation, and excellence that also encourages learning and development. Energy is contagious. Both positive and negative energy. However, the most impactful leaders have a contagious positive energy, which is the type of energy that uplifts, encourages, and renews others.[9] It is a type of energy that is magnetic. It is here where the greatest impact will be born, not just for your generation, but for the next.

How Do We Enhance Our "I" in the Global G.R.I.T. System™?

To achieve the "I" in the Global G.R.I.T. System™ means to be motivated by something far more significant than personal gain. It requires creating positive change in others. This creates a significant impact, not just in teams or within organizations, but in the lives of those around you, including your community. It is a catalyst that propels not just you, but everyone around you toward their pinnacle of potential.

Techniques That Help Enhance the "I" in the Global G.R.I.T. System™

- **Identify Your Purpose:** No, I don't mean the purpose of the company you work for or own, I am talking about your individual purpose. What's the reason you get out of bed every day? Who is it that you are impacting, even if it is in your personal life? What's the reason you do what you do? If you struggle to answer this question, I recommend you take time to really think about it—write down words on a piece of paper that resonate with who you are and what you want to achieve in your lifetime. Spend time with others who inspire you and write down why they inspire you.

- **Storytelling:** The way we articulate our visions and share our experiences has the power to impact others. Resonating with your team and others through storytelling and providing insights into your experience that many can relate to or feel affected by can spark inspiration.

- **Authenticity:** Nothing impacts people more deeply than genuine connection. Authentic leadership, devoid of any facade, invites others into a space of trust and inspiration. Authenticity is not about showcasing perfection, it's about unveiling a journey marked by highs and lows, replete with lessons and filled with inspiration. When authenticity is at the forefront, team members and employees show higher personal initiative and are more engaged at work. This leads to innovative solutions implemented across the organization.[10] So be open about your own journey, including the setbacks you've overcome. Authenticity has a ripple effect, it encourages others to pursue their own paths with courage.

- **Empathy:** A leader's empathy quotient often determines the depth of their impact.[11] Through targeted empathy-building exercises, you not only understand but feel what your teams and others are going through, thereby laying the groundwork for inspiration.

- **Measuring Impact:** You can implement metrics with impact scorecards and identify how you are encouraging others to help quantify the intangible yet essential aspects of inspiration and impact.

- **Mentorship Programs:** Theory is the foundation, but practice is the key to mastery. Providing opportunities for practical application through mentor-mentee relationships can be incredibly potent for honing the skill of impacting and inspiring others.

- **Technology:** Leveraging digital platforms can assist in real-time monitoring and encouraging behaviors that inspire and impact.

- **Branding Yourself:** Impact isn't confined to the close quarters of a conference room. How you present yourself publicly can significantly elevate your potential for broader impact and inspiration and create trust by demonstrating your authenticity on a universal level.

- **Community:** Engage in social projects and get involved in community activities or social causes. Use your platform to speak about them. Such initiatives offer a multi-faceted environment where your capacity to inspire can be both tested and honed as well as bringing out the aspect of the "I" in the Global G.R.I.T. System™ outside of the immediate organizational context.

- **Culture:** Creating a culture that encourages feedback from diverse perspectives and has a recurring exchange of ideas ensures a continual cycle of growth with constant upgrades to your inspiration and impact.

- **Communication:** Have meaningful conversations that have the power to change perspectives. Use your words to inspire change and listen to others—really listen to what they are saying rather than thinking about the next thing you want to say.

- **Collaboration Over Competition:** When team members feel their contributions are valued it creates an impact that enhances the capacity to learn and encourages innovation.[12]
- **Provide Autonomy:** Giving team members the freedom to choose how they accomplish their work improves their sense of control and ownership. It also leads to greater creativity, innovation, and job satisfaction.[13]

By applying each of these techniques you will enrich your own impact reservoir and also elevate those around you in a meaningful, lasting way. However, this requires constant learning, experimentation, and encouragement of creativity within teams. It is critical to provide opportunities for team members to learn and develop in new areas. One way to do this is through encouraging professional development and providing opportunities for team members to develop new skills, take on new challenges, and advance their career as part of the "I" in the Global G.R.I.T. System™. This can include investing in training, mentoring, and coaching. Anthony Mirabile of Goldman Sachs conveyed this point masterfully when he said, "When you spend money, it's gone. When you invest money, you expect a return. Invest in your people."

Why We Need the "I" in the Global G.R.I.T. System™

Innovators are the engines of a company, driving it forward by continually coming up with fresh ideas and unique approaches. Innovation leads to the development of different services, products, or processes that can lead to a competitive advantage. The ability to differentiate is critical for long-term success. It also leads to improved experiences by clients, which increases loyalty and encourages repeat business. Additionally, it attracts talent. People are attracted to environments that have a reputation for innovation,[14] which will aid in retaining top talent. Subsequently, innovators encourage a culture of curiosity and continual learning, which has a ripple effect across the entire organization. They typically question the status quo and encourage a culture to ask "why" and "how" to increase fresh thinking in others as they look ahead, which is essential for a business to thrive and sustain long-term growth because they can think about what's next and identify potential risks as well as opportunities.[15] Milwaukee Tools is a prime example of this innovative behavior, having grown 20 times over the past 15 years as they foresee market trends and shifts in customer behavior, which is how they have been able to grow rapidly, on a pace to double the company over the next decade. One of the major ways they have achieved this is by living with one simple principle: "We don't follow markets, we lead them" (Paul Richardson, SVP, Milwaukee Tools). This is a company with innovators in leadership, which encourages employees and team members to think differently and unleash their creativity, which in turn encourages innovation. Understanding and using the "I" in your grit creates a ripple effect throughout the entire organization and impacts others on a tremendous level. Another example is Elon Musk. SpaceX and Tesla alone have shifted industries to change and adapt. The innovation of Tesla has pushed the automotive industry toward sustainable energy solutions while SpaceX's accomplishments, including reusable rockets, have made the concept of commercial space travel a genuine possibility. Innovation is an organizational asset but how we get there is through the "I" in your grit.

Innovators don't just adapt to change, they are often the ones instigating it. When leaders give their teams the autonomy and resources they need, it often sparks creative thinking and novel approaches to problem-solving, which leads to innovation. As leaders, we have the responsibility and privilege of providing guidance and support to those around us. By being persistent, focusing on teamwork, and creating a supportive environment, we can have a significant impact on the growth and development of individuals and, ultimately, our organizations. Motivation is one of the most critical factors that impact individual and team performance.[16] And how do we create motivation in others? If you recall back to the process outlined in Chapter 5, it is through creating belief. Being an impactful leader requires constant learning, experimentation, and encouraging creativity within teams. It's important to provide opportunities for team members to learn and develop in new areas, fail, and grow.

Authentic leadership strengthens the emotional bond employees have with their organization, which in turn enhances their creative abilities and ultimately boosts their performance, resulting in tremendous impact.[17]

"As a leader you need to invest time in others by being visible to them and allowing them to be visible to you," Anthony Mirabile told me. "It is up to the leader to unlock the value that is within each of the others that you are counting on to help pursue the organizational goal," he said.

"Insider status" directly impacts the innovation of team members. Additionally, team member exchange and servant leadership are directly correlated to perceived insider status.[18] It is vital to have team member exchange to generate trust, open communication, and reciprocity among the team. This will create impact in the following areas: enhanced team cohesion, increased job satisfaction, higher productivity across the organization, and ultimately innovation and problem solving ideas. This will develop mutual respect owing to an understanding between team members, often leading to an improved collaboration. The concept of team member exchange is important for understanding how relationships among team members can influence individual and collective outcomes within an organization. "Insider status" for employees can be achieved by carrying out team member exchange and impacting others through servant leadership, encouraging employee development through coaching, working alongside team members if a tight deadline approaches, and empowering others to take ownership related to their tasks. This in turn will aid in the team member having a sense of belonging and not feeling like an outsider, which leads to an emotional investment for the success of the team and the entire organization. This develops trust and respect, which leads to increased job satisfaction, belief, and motivation.[19] Furthermore, the perception that one's opinion and efforts have an impact on team and organizational outcomes means they perceive that they have influence. This unlocks the innovation needed for a company to have long-term viability.[20] When team members feel more committed to their work you will see increased engagement, reduced turnover, and higher productivity.[21]

Why Do Some of Us Struggle With the "I" in the Global G.R.I.T. System™?

Innovators are typically outgoing and talkative and some of us are naturally more introverted and not as talkative. It takes great energy to be an innovator, but if you struggle to pull from your "I" in the Global

G.R.I.T. System™ when needed in situations, you must put yourself in environments where you can practice the various techniques to enhance this pillar, especially if you are in a leadership role. Also adopting the five pillars I outlined in Chapter 3 from a personal standpoint will enhance your energy levels and open up the creative part of your thinking.

Your behavior as a leader or as a team member in an organization has a direct correlation to the motivation and work of others.[22] You may struggle with pulling from the "I" in the Global G.R.I.T. System™ if you have a lack of self-awareness about how your actions and words affect others. Having a fear of failure can also hold you back from pulling from your "I" in the Global G.R.I.T. System™. Being afraid of making mistakes can paralyze creativity and discourage innovation. You will be less likely to take the risks necessary to innovate as a result of having a fear of failure.[23] Your skill set in areas such as communication, empathy, and active listening—all critical elements for inspiring and impacting others—may need to be enhanced if your environment doesn't provide you the opportunity to do so. Remember the purpose as a technique to help enhance your ability to impact others? Well, if you lack in this area and do not have a clear vision and purpose, it will be incredibly difficult for you to inspire others. Best put, vision and purpose act as the magnetic force that attracts people to a cause.

Take a look at the culture around you, not just at work but in your personal life. Do you have the culture of excellence I described in prior chapters? If not, this may be discouraging innovation and thus affecting you negatively, which means you are having a negative impact on others. If you are suffering from burnout or emotional fatigue you might find it difficult to muster the energy to inspire or impact others, because you yourself may be struggling to sustain your own motivation. So too can psychological factors affect your ability to inspire and impact others. Low self-esteem, insecurity, or even past traumas can create mental barriers that prevent you from impacting others effectively.[24]

By dissecting each of these aspects you not only set the stage for your own growth but also contribute to an environment that empowers everyone around you to be more innovative and impactful. And when it comes to the "I" in the Global G.R.I.T. System™, understanding the barriers can provide valuable insights into how to overcome them and turn into crucial aspects for leaders who not only lead but also inspire and make a lasting impact.

If You Are the "I" in the Global G.R.I.T. System™

If your Grit Type Indicator™ shows your dominance as an innovator, this means you are a natural storyteller, you are easy to talk to, you have a great presence, you are energized, creative, enthusiastic, and focused on people and relationships rather than tasks. You see the possibilities, are extremely creative, and love to help others become excited by their potential. You are fast-paced and typically make decisions from your gut rather than making the decision based on logic alone. You are the one who innovates, creates, and inspires others, because you have the capacity to see what others do best and how to match individuals to specific tasks. You handle the unexpected well and can paint the picture for others. You love to brainstorm, you learn quickly, and you are generous with your praise. Your dominance as an innovator makes you an integral part of the team. The company needs individuals like you to inspire and impact others to create the belief, which in turn creates the motivation, which influences cognition and alters brain processes, which then leads to the adoption of a growth mindset to carry out the very task needed to achieve the goal. It is also important to recognize when you also need to pull from other areas of your grit. Such as the G, R, and the T. This creates equity in your grit and leads your team to understand all areas of the Global G.R.I.T. System™ and develop all four pillars.

Impact on others is critical in leadership because leaders are not just responsible for achieving their goals but also for their team's success and well-being. Leaders have the power to influence the culture of their organization and inspire their team to strive for greatness. They can also influence in a negative way if they do not demonstrate the "I" in the Global G.R.I.T. System™ in a powerful and confident manner. It is crucial, therefore, that measurements of the impact across the organization are carried out to identify whether leadership behavior is impacting in a positive way and if that is leading to increased innovation and motivation across the company.

Learning Points From the "I" in the Global G.R.I.T. System™

Remember, the "innovators" have great focus and energy in the moment, as long as they are being true to who they are and genuinely enjoy what they are doing. They hunt by learning quickly, improve with every step they take and learn from failure. They are divergent thinkers and able to go with the flow should something suddenly change. They are comfortable in times of change, have an agile mind, are articulate, optimistic, and easy to get along with. They make friends quickly, regardless if you are the competition. The "I's" can make friends with their prey, and are excellent collaborators as a result. They sometimes, however, put too much trust into others, which can make them vulnerable to being hunted, which is why the other pillars of the Global G.R.I.T. System™ are so crucial for the "I" to work effectively as the hunter. Remember, as Anthony Mirabile said, "Confidence is contagious." Why is impacting others essential for a leader? Impacting others creates the belief, which in turn generates the motivation needed to eventually unlock the innovation in others, which is critical for long-term sustained success of an organization. Motivated teams tend to perform better, have higher job satisfaction levels, and lower absenteeism rates.[25] A motivated team also helps to create a positive and productive work environment and can set the foundation for the organization's culture. A leader's role in impacting team members and employees is crucial because it ensures that the team is working toward common goals. This generates individual and team growth, increases job satisfaction, which increases engagement, and fosters a culture of innovation, which results in organizational success.

As a leader, the impact we have on others and in our organization is a crucial element of our success and personal development. However, it's not just about achieving personal success. Rather, it's about impacting others. This truly demonstrates leadership, fosters a culture of creativity and innovation, and embodies the grit mentality.

*"The greatest leader is not necessarily
the one who does the greatest things.
He is the one that gets the people
to do the greatest things."*

Ronald Reagan

10 Key Leadership Lessons From This Chapter:

- To achieve the "I" in the Global G.R.I.T. System™ means to be motivated by something far more significant than personal gain.

- Impacting others positively creates belief and thus motivation, which influences cognition and alters brain patterns, allowing teams to work together toward shared goals.

- The most impactful leaders have a contagious positive energy.

- Your behavior as a leader or as a team member in an organization is directly correlated to the motivation and work of others.

- Motivation is one of the most critical factors that impacts individual and team performance.

- Vision and purpose act as the magnetic force that attracts people to a cause. You need to be clear with your individual purpose in order to inspire others and ultimately impact them positively, which will lead to increased innovation across the company, which is needed in order to have sustained growth.

- Impacting others creates the belief, which eventually unlocks the innovation in others, and is critical for long-term sustained success of the organization.

- A motivated team helps create a positive and productive work environment and can set the foundation for the organization's culture, leading to additional innovation.

- Innovators hunt by learning quickly, improving every step they take and learning from failure. They are divergent thinkers and able to go with the flow should something suddenly change. They can sometimes be too trusting, resulting in a swift and sudden change in roles of being the "hunter" to suddenly becoming the "hunted". Awareness of this is critical and it is also a reason why pulling from the other areas of grit in the Global G.R.I.T. System™ is needed in combination with the "I."

- Strategies and more regimented schedules can help innovators stay in the role of the "hunter." However, do not cage their surroundings too small, for this will kill their innovation, which will cause their belief to decline.

CHAPTER 9

Take Responsibility:

The "T" in the Global G.R.I.T. System™

---

*"Your life is the fruit of your own doing.
You have no one to blame but yourself."*

Joseph Campbell

TAKE RESPONSIBILITY: Why it's Part of the Grit Mentality

There are three types of responsibility as outlined by Gerald Dworkin:[1]

- Causal Responsibility
- Liability Responsibility
- Role Responsibility

"Causal responsibility" arises when a result can be directly linked to your actions. However, this doesn't automatically imply "liability responsibility," which entails being held accountable for your behavior. It's not just about the actions you took but also about whether you should be held answerable for the outcomes of those actions. This type of responsibility evaluates the ethics and legality of one's behavior, taking into account factors like intent, foreseeability, and due diligence. There are situations where your actions could be unavoidable or consequences unforeseeable. "Role responsibility" pertains to the obligations or areas that fall under your purview due to the role you hold. Ensuring specific outcomes either occur or are prevented based on the tasks assigned to you is known as "Task Responsibility".[2] These types of responsibility often intersect and overlap, but understanding their nuances allows for more targeted approaches in leadership, ethical decision-making, and organizational management.

Taking responsibility impacts almost every facet of leadership, including team dynamics and morale, as well as long-term strategic and sustainable success. It builds trust with each other but also builds trust within ourselves. The journey to building trust starts remarkably early; it begins in the initial stages of our life. From the moment we are born we enter into relationships that form the bedrock of our understanding of trust and responsibility. As babies, we trust our parents or caregivers to meet our needs, setting the stage for how we give and receive trust throughout our lives. It is a basic human need that doesn't ever stop;[3] it only evolves and becomes more intricate as we grow, taking on new dimensions in professional settings. Our fundamental human need for trust, intertwined into our earliest experiences, underscores its importance in achieving sustainable success in leadership.

Just as responsibility shapes the trust and integrity within a team and within ourselves, grit strengthens our resolve to tackle challenges head-on. When we cultivate grit proactively, by choosing to engage with difficult tasks and nurturing resilience, we are not just preparing ourselves for success, but also equipping ourselves to deal with failure in a constructive manner. This synergistic relationship between responsibility and grit serves as a catalyst, pushing us to rise from setbacks and transforming us into leaders who can navigate the unpredictable waters of adversity without spiraling into negativity, which we already know from Chapter 7 we easily do, owing to the negativity bias.[4]

The very essence of choosing our own grit, as discussed in Chapter 1, involves a willingness to take on challenges and work through them, so when grit chooses us, we are more equipped to handle adversity in a way that will not send us into a negative spiral. This means we will face failure before we reach success. When failures come (and they will), it is critical to accept the responsibility of the feelings and emotions attached to those failures. Why? So we can recognize the reaction of that feeling and accept it, but understand that we can choose how we look at it by taking responsibility for our actions, refining them, learning from them, and becoming better as a result, which leads to success. In other words, taking responsibility facilitates a learning environment. It allows you to identify what went wrong, adjust your strategy, and persevere. Additionally, when you take responsibility you confront adversity head-on, rather than deflecting or blaming others. This is how you build resilience.

One of the most important aspects of taking responsibility includes building trust with others. When you take responsibility for your actions, you show that you are accountable. Your team members and others around you are much more likely to trust you when you own up to your mistakes and identify the steps needed to take to rectify them. Additionally, by admitting your faults or mistakes, you present yourself as a genuine, transparent individual. Authenticity develops deeper connections and thus trust.[5] Leadership that exhibits taking responsibility tends to attract trust and loyalty. In essence, leaders who take responsibility for their actions command respect. They are more effective in motivating their teams because when a mistake happens, they are quick to own up, finding a solution rather than getting stuck on the problem. This speeds up the problem-solving process and shows adaptability, a crucial trait in today's fast-paced environment.

In leadership specifically, it is essential to take responsibility for one's own actions before expecting it from others. You have to be the role model for your team members, which will lead to an increase in this behavior from others. In doing so, it shows others how you hold yourself accountable, which creates accountability in others. You are creating a culture of responsibility, where actions are deliberate and thoughtful, reducing impulsive behavior. However, it is important to note that there are times where impulsive behavior is appropriate and can lead to incredible opportunities, which is why it is essential to develop all four pillars of the Global G.R.I.T. System™ and not just rely on one during times of adversity. Taking responsibility helps you identify your own strengths and weaknesses and sets the foundation for growth. It builds credibility and provides belief in others that you are reliable, which leads team members to be motivated (see the process outlined in Chapter 5). Furthermore, by taking responsibility you can help resolve conflicts both in the workplace and in your personal life by building trust. This helps de-escalate situations and leads to more constructive conversations about solutions.[6]

Taking responsibility can be empowering. You are taking control by acknowledging your behavior that can either lead to positive or negative outcomes, which means you understand the power behind your decisions, fully appreciating the consequences of your action or inaction. This puts you in control of your life and in doing so, you gain self-awareness, which leads to growth. When you understand your leadership style you can make the necessary adjustments.

Subsequently, on a societal level, personal responsibility is crucial for social cohesion and stability. When you take responsibility for your actions, it leads to a more balanced and harmonious community. It also contributes to ethical integrity and reflects character, a trait that's admired and respected by others. This is a crucial point as leaders are the ones who set the ethical tone for the organization.

It has been found that over time, taking responsibility contributes to long-term success,[7] both personally and as a leader in the workplace.

It sends a strong message to the team. This can be motivating for team members and helps maintain high morale, as it shows the leader is with the team. This in turn yields considerable influence that extends beyond your immediate team. You are actually contributing to a broader culture of accountability and ethical conduct, creating trust, loyalty, and reliability that extends beyond the walls of your company. Trust is the cornerstone of any meaningful relationship, whether it is personal or professional, so having the "T" in the Global G.R.I.T. System™ is essential to set the standard for others to create high performing teams.

Sarah Powell, CEO of Performance Physio, PLLC, is an academic in the field of performance physiotherapy, including completing a fellowship at the American Academy of Orthopedic Manual Therapy. She sat down with me to explain that a big part of taking responsibility is to be humble in the process of using your grit to face adversity. She said, "If you set a goal in life, and you really want it, you have to own it; if you do, you will achieve it. But if you don't take ownership, and set the standard for yourself, you start to drift and your goal will subside. It is about having a continual pursuit of excellence without wavering, but if you don't take responsibility for your actions, you will never get there."

An example of this is when I injured myself through intense training, and had muscle fatigue during one of the workouts with my fellow athletes. Instead of listening to my body, I chose to carry on to finish the workout, because I did not want to let my team down. The consequences of those actions led to many weeks of physio (with Sarah Powell), owing to a neck and shoulder injury, which resulted in constant nerve pain and numbness. With a competition not far off, it was a risk to continue training at the level I was used to. I had to focus on the long game, which is a full recovery. I had to learn how to be humble in my decision to cage the lioness during training sessions, opting to modify movements and scale the weight while my neck and shoulder were healing. I had to take responsibility for my actions. Had I not taken responsibility, I would have had to pull out of the competition and probably would have needed surgery at some point. Instead of focusing on short-term goals, I listened to my body and focused on the long-term goals. It takes strength to be humble to lower oneself from a constant high level of energy. Go-getters in the Grit Type Indicator™ will typically have the toughest time focusing on this type of responsibility. "If you try to fight the nervous system, which is the main computer processing system of your body, you will lose and the nervous system will always win if you irritate it," Sarah Powell told me. Thus, by taking responsibility, I learned how to be humble when navigating this curveball, getting injured weeks out from a worldwide competition I had committed to with my fellow athletes. To help with this, the "R" in the Global G.R.I.T. System™ helps with the "T" in the Global G.R.I.T. System™ to realize that "No pain, no gain" is not helpful to an injured athlete who may be dominant in the "G" in the Global G.R.I.T. System™. Sarah said that learning how to change your psychology to calm the symptoms so you can actually get to where you want to go, especially for the go-getters, is essential and will help reduce frustration tremendously.

I've personally learned a lot through taking responsibility and listening to my body. The most valuable lessons actually come from learning through adversity. It's why choosing your grit is incredibly important, particularly for practical learners, because you will learn by experiencing it. So you have to choose your grit before it chooses you to harness the "T" in your grit. And if grit has already chosen you, go back to what you learned with the "T" in the Global G.R.I.T. System™.

How Do We Enhance our "T" in the Global G.R.I.T. System™?

Taking responsibility is not just about owning up to your decisions and actions, it's about self-awareness, transparency, and courageous action. Leaders who take ownership don't just acknowledge their mistakes, they actively seek to remedy them, demonstrating a commitment to personal growth and team well-being. It is built on a foundation of vulnerability and a willingness to strip away the ego and face the difficult truth. It's about standing in the arena, even when the outcomes are not guaranteed. This intentional approach to responsibility establishes trust and creates the way for open dialogue, eliminating the destructive cycle of blame and defensiveness. By taking responsibility, you empower yourself but also those around you to be resilient, adaptable, and purpose-driven.

Techniques That Help Enhance the "T" in the Global G.R.I.T. System™

- **Self-Assessment:** Reflect on a past situation where you avoided responsibility. Identify and write down the emotions or thoughts that led to this behavior of evading responsibility:

_____

_____

_____

_____

_____

_____

_____

- **Value Alignment:** Examine and write down your core values and see how they align with taking responsibility. If there's a mismatch, it's time to revisit what you truly stand for:

_____

_____

_____

_____

_____

_____

_____

- **Active Listening:** Practice listening to feedback without getting defensive. This opens the door for constructive criticism, which is crucial for taking responsibility.

- **Emotional Intelligence:** Work on emotional self-regulation and empathy. Being aware of your emotions and those of others makes it easier to own your actions and understand their impact.

- **Accountability Partners:** Surround yourself with people who are good at taking responsibility and ask them to hold you accountable, through mentors, coaches, and other leaders.

- **Set Small Goals:** If you find taking responsibility challenging, start with small, manageable tasks, outlined in Chapter 1. Owning the smaller tasks fully will set the stage for handling bigger challenges.

- **Avoid Blame-shifting:** Catch yourself each time you find yourself blaming someone or something else for your actions. Stop and redirect the focus back on yourself.

- **Be Direct and Honest:** When you make a mistake, own up to it **immediately**. Honesty is a large piece of the foundation for responsibility.

- **Offer Solutions:** Taking responsibility also means being part of the solution. When you admit to a mistake, also propose ways to make things right.

- **Self-Review:** Regularly evaluate your actions to see how well you're doing at taking responsibility. Celebrate your successes and learn from your failures. You may need a mentor or coach to help guide your self-review as we are prone to negativity bias. Ensure you have one.

- **Seek Feedback:** Don't be afraid to ask for external input on how well you're doing in terms of responsibility. This can provide invaluable insights.

Taking responsibility is an ongoing process, not a one-time event. It takes time, patience, and a willingness to grow and change. The journey of how we get to our end goal can change the very path we are on and can change the end goal in positive ways.

Why We Need the "T" in the Global G.R.I.T. System™

I put myself through severe pain every single day. Why? *Accountability*. As a leader, I take ownership in every area of my life. I work with a team in all aspects of my life, every day. My family, my fellow athletes, my company, my military tribe, my clients, my network, my friends. They are all my team and I wouldn't be where I am today without them. How do I do it? I remain accountable for my own actions and I hold others accountable for theirs. If one of my "teams" does not succeed in an area where we wanted to flourish, I do not blame others, I look to myself to say, "What could I have done better? What can I do next time that will provide different results?

What can I work on to get better to be a stronger support for the team?" As a leader, I take on this responsibility.

The "T" in the Global G.R.I.T. System™ is indispensable in both life and leadership. It serves as a compelling call to action for us to inspire others to harvest a similar culture of this part of grit in their own lives, extending beyond the confines of the workplace.[8] Without taking responsibility, you will only go so far if you are a go-getter, reframer, or innovator as defined by the Grit Type Indicator™. The behavior you exhibit sets the standard for those around you. If you're responsible, your team is likely to imitate this trait, thus boosting morale and increasing productivity.

Acknowledging mistakes and learning from them contributes to personal development as it also helps create trust in those around you if you are consistent at taking responsibility for all of your actions.[9] Also, taking responsibility results in better decision making. If a project that has been carried out by your team under your leadership fails, the commitment of the failed project escalates. Escalation decisions are faster than de-escalation decisions because of the network in our brain that is recruited for escalation when the outcome is viewed as negative versus positive.[10] However, taking responsibility provides a sense of ownership and control, because when you feel in control, you are more likely to be engaged and effective both inside and outside of the workplace.[11] It will also allow for problem-solving to be a proactive behavior, and thus others will see you as a leader who is highly regarded, which in turn opens up opportunities for your leadership journey and for the overall organizational productivity.

Contrary to popular belief, findings from research indicate that taking responsibility can actually reduce stress.[12] When you stop avoiding or deflecting responsibility, the tension that comes from procrastination and denial is reduced and in some cases eliminated. You feel an increase in self-esteem and satisfaction because you face your responsibilities head on, which in turn creates the belief and thus the motivation to influence your cognition and alter your brain patterns. Then you can cultivate a positive attitude toward a growth mindset, which allows you to adopt the "T" in the Global G.R.I.T. System™, thus providing you with more courage to take on harder challenges and take responsibility for the outcome, whether positive or negative. Ultimately, taking responsibility contributes to personal growth and helps improve our relationships with others, both inside and outside of the workplace. It enhances your decision-making capabilities, and impacts others by creating a culture of accountability. On a societal level, taking responsibility is crucial for social cohesion and stability. When you take responsibility for your actions, it leads to a more cordial community and peaceful team setting with reduced conflict. Subsequently, by accepting the consequences of your decisions, you are creating an environment where others have the belief that taking responsibility is the culture they need to create. This motivates them to work collaboratively, ultimately elevating not just individual performance but the team, resulting in an organizational shift and thus, positive change. Taking responsibility for your actions serves as a powerful model for others around you, and directly influences the emotional investment employees have in their roles within the organization, leading to a high performing team which results in greater productivity.[13]

Why Do Some of Us Struggle with the "T" in the Global G.R.I.T. System™?

If you have ever had your trust broken, you know how difficult it is to regain it. Whether you realize it or not, your brain has programmed you to be more cautious around others as a result. If you find yourself to be controlling or others perceive you as wanting to always control a situation, odds are you have a severe lack of trust in others. Thus, when your trust is betrayed you may try to control others in order to not be harmed.[14] If you find yourself unable to control the situation or the people involved, you may feel threatened by withdrawing from interaction. The result of this is that you become incredibly independent and self-reliant, to the point of shutting off your emotions and keeping your distance if someone is pleasant toward you.[15] It is important to highlight times when your trust has been broken in the workplace and in your personal life. Then evaluate how that has impacted your thoughts of others, perhaps even altered your relationships with others as a result.

Write down a time when your trust was broken and how that contributed to you controlling a situation or a person or shutting down and retreating from that person or situation.

Time when your trust was broken:

_____

_____

_____

_____

How that impacted you since:

_____

_____

_____

_____

By not taking responsibility you are prohibiting yourself from developing your abilities. If you cannot take responsibility and cannot trust yourself to do something, then you are reinforcing that message to your brain and it will "protect you" from what it recognizes as inevitable failure. You'll rely on others, instead of yourself, and allow others to control you, meaning you can become easily manipulated, because you believe other people know better than you and you won't challenge the status quo.

Trusting too much and trusting too little, in others, can be damaging.[16] When you trust someone completely, you may find yourself willing to accept their setting limits on your behavior. This can be detrimental to your own standards if they create a belief in you that does not align with your culture of excellence.

When you trust too little, you may withdraw from others, which in leadership is detrimental to the team dynamics. It will lead to reduced collaboration because you are reluctant to share ideas and resources. This can hinder innovation and problem-solving, leading to increased conflict.[17] It can also lead to disengagement among the team and reduced morale, which in turn may affect productivity. Ultimately, this will lead to higher turnover, because a workplace without trust misses opportunities to value the strengths in team members. Distrust also slows down decision-making abilities. When you can't trust others to act, every small decision becomes a bottleneck, reducing overall effectiveness.[18]

If you trust too little, you may find that you micromanage, losing out on the potential benefits of delegation, such as the development of team capabilities and skills. All of this adds to increased stress, isolation, and a reduction in your grit. It also impacts all the other areas of your grit in the Global G.R.I.T. System™. If you have a lack of trust in yourself, you are unlikely to get tasks done because you don't believe in yourself. Moreover, you will question your reframing of situations, owing to not trusting yourself with the thoughts surrounding the reframe techniques. Additionally, a lack of trust in others will impact your level of inspiration, as it will be challenging if you can't trust your team to execute on your shared vision. Trusting too little can be a significant roadblock in your efforts to build and equally be a part of a high-performing team. It could limit not only your leadership effectiveness but also the collective potential of everyone around you.

Other reasons why some of us struggle with the "T" in the Global G.R.I.T. System™ are due to psychological factors. A fear of consequences can result in avoiding responsibility and lead to either inaction or the wrong action. This includes CEOs who might be fired from their high-paying positions if they acknowledge their role in a failure.[19]

Perfectionism is also a contributor as individuals who exhibit those traits find it difficult to admit mistakes, viewing them as personal failures rather than learning experiences. The "R" in the Global G.R.I.T. System™ will strengthen the "T."

Emotional factors come into play too, with our inability to harness the "T" in the Global G.R.I.T. System™. Some individuals may be naturally defensive when criticized, owing to past experiences, making it difficult for them to accept responsibility. Furthermore, social and cultural factors can affect your ability to take responsibility. The way you were raised plays a significant role. If your parents or caregiver shielded you from responsibility or consequences, you may struggle with these concepts as an adult. Social norms may also discourage taking responsibility. A workplace culture that punishes mistakes versus using them as learning experience may result in team members being less likely to take responsibility.

One of the main culprits in organizations that have issues with employees, leaders, and team members not taking responsibility is a lack of systems in place to hold everyone accountable. Without accountability mechanisms, it is easy for individuals to avoid responsibility. Additionally, those who may act on impulse, in either a high stress or high emotion state, may find it difficult to take responsibility for their actions.

Cognitive bias also comes into play with struggles to take responsibility, such as attributing positive outcomes to your own actions and negative outcomes to external factors. "Cognitive dissonance" is a psychological theory that refers to the mental battle one has when their actions conflict with their beliefs or values.[20] For example, if you value health but you eat food that is bad for you. The cognitive dissonance between your belief and action might lead you to quit eating processed foods or to downplay the health risks associated with eating such foods. Sometimes, rather than changing beliefs or actions, you might add new beliefs to justify or rationalize your inconsistency.

As leaders, it is critical to be aware of your cognitive dissonance, if it exists, as it will affect decision making. It can lead to suboptimal choices, as people might overlook contradictory information to reduce discomfort. When mergers and acquisitions take place, cognitive dissonance can be prevalent due to a change in organizational culture or new strategies that conflict with existing beliefs or practices within the organization. It is at this moment that the "T" in the Global G.R.I.T. System™ needs to be abundant. Leaders who recognize cognitive dissonance can address it constructively, using it as an opportunity for dialogue, reflection, and growth, both for themselves and their teams.

If You Are the "T" in the Global G.R.I.T. System™

If your Grit Type Indicator™ shows your dominance as a Trustworthy Titan, this means you know how to grow talent in others and build productive teams. You see the strengths and talents in others. You have a calming influence on others as others see you as being trustworthy, likable, loyal, and personable. You know how to create trust in others, and you may find yourself having deep relationships with a small circle. You are dependable and consistent in your approach and have a fair and just way in your treatment of others. You can often see how people who are very different in their approach can work together because you see the potential in others and have an instinctive understanding of those around you. Aside from consistency and dependability as your hallmarks in leadership, underscored by your commitment to treating everyone with fairness and equity, your skill set also includes a unique capacity for identifying synergies among people with divergent approaches. You see potential where others might see conflict, and your instinctive understanding of human behavior positions you as a mediator or, as many would say, a "bridge-builder" within the organization. In an environment where divisiveness may occur, your skill for bringing together varied groups stands out as a valued leadership quality. This ability does more than just generate admiration, it harbors a level of trust, devotion, and a sense of collective success within the team.

Taking responsibility is vital in leadership because your role as a leader extends beyond your own accomplishments to encompass the success and well-being of your team. As a leader, you wield the power to shape the organizational culture and inspire your team toward excellence. However, you can also have a detrimental influence if you don't embody the "T" in the Global G R I T System™ with conviction and credibility. For this reason, it's essential to conduct assessments across the organization to gauge whether leadership behavior is positively affecting trust and reliability. Moreover, these assessments can help determine if the presence of a "Trustworthy Titan" at the helm is leading to a more responsible and engaged workforce.

Learning Points From the "T" in the Global G.R.I.T. System™

Taking responsibility in everything you do is critical for the development of not just you, but those around you. If you have children, remember they are always watching your behavior and actions. If you do not take responsibility for your actions, your children are unlikely to either.[21] It is the same in the workplace. As a leader or aspiring leader, everything you do is being watched by others. You need to set an example and set the standard to build a culture of accountability.

Anthony Mirable agrees that the grit you choose is a lifestyle. We can only achieve this through discipline, and discipline requires grit. Specifically the "T" in the Global G.R.I.T. System™. Anthony Mirable said that, "Very few people are willing to do the things that it takes to be great because it is very hard to do those things on a consistent basis and it is through that discipline and consistency that you not only train your body and your mind but you seek out opportunities so that your newfound set of muscles do not decline. Embrace the failure." This revolves around the critical importance of discipline and consistency in the pursuit of greatness. It emphasizes that achieving high levels of success is not a one-time effort but a continuous journey requiring unshakeable commitment. The consistency in your actions trains both your mind and body, preparing you to seize new opportunities and maintain your progress. The barrier to greatness is often the inability to sustain the effort and discipline needed, making those who can do so a rare and exceptional breed. If we take responsibility, more people around us will be able to achieve the discipline needed to achieve greatness, not just for ourselves, but for others.

Additionally, harnessing the "T" in the Global G.R.I.T. System™ also allows for the "I" in the system to increase. Thomas Watson Sr. (IBM) said, "The fastest way to success is to double your failure rate".[22] In other words, invention is born from the crucible of failure and a company won't achieve groundbreaking innovation unless it fosters a culture that not only embraces risk-taking but also values the lessons extracted from ensuing missteps, which involves taking responsibility.

Confidence can be gained by taking responsibility,[23] and as a leader, the whole team will come together and be unified to work together to strategize, solve problems, and provide solutions for each other's success. If confidence is lost in a leader, the opposite effect will happen and cracks will appear. Like a dam under pressure, the leader will fall, the dam will explode, and the team will dissolve. So own your circumstance. Just like Micky Ward, the former welterweight champion did. He told me that in his mid to late twenties he took control of his actions. He needed to make a change in order to progress, so he "got rid" of a lot of people around him. He wanted to build his "culture of excellence." He took responsibility and that helped him in his journey to becoming the welterweight champion.

Taking responsibility is an undeniable cornerstone of leadership, but it's important to recognize that this act does more than just enforce accountability, it also cultivates trust, a critical currency in any relationship. Bipul Sinha, CEO of Rubrik, encapsulates this idea when he says, "Trust is not based on knowledge, it's based on authenticity".[24] In the realm of leadership, taking responsibility enhances your authenticity. When leaders are authentic in owning their actions, they lay down a foundation of trust that is not built on the mere accumulation of facts or achievements but on the genuine human connection that comes from being transparent and consistent. This authentic trust not only fortifies relationships within a team but also strengthens the leaders' confidence in themselves, setting the stage for resilience, grit, and ultimately, sustainable success.

The disciplined "Hunter" that comes with the "T" in the Global G.R.I.T. System™ doesn't have the erratic movements or impulsive behaviors often associated with aggressive hunting styles. Instead, they have a consistent approach, long-term focus, and a determined commitment to ethical conduct and accountability, which makes them predictable. Team members know what to expect and find stability in this consistency. However, being too predictable may tip off the "prey," letting opportunities slip away. That's where the other elements of the Global G.R.I.T. System™ come to the rescue, injecting just the right dose of unpredictability to keep the hunter from being hunted. The Trustworthy Titans are the silent hunters. They are the ones you don't even realize are hunting, but if they become too predictable, with their stable approach, they run the risk of becoming hunted. They need the support of all areas of the Global G.R.I.T. System™ to ensure that they remain as the hunters.

By taking responsibility, it will give you the strength and the confidence for others to see that you can take back the power to focus on the end goal for the team and overcome the powerlessness that comes from being a "victim" in a given situation that in your eyes may have failed. Instead, it allows you to work together with your team, and move through any given situation, but it all starts with accountability. Accountability starts with taking responsibility, and taking responsibility starts today.

Own it.

Apply it.

Do it.

*"The best way to make a difference
in the world is to start by making
a difference in your own life."*

Robyn Benincasa

10 Key Leadership Lessons From This Chapter:

- There are three types of responsibility: Causal Responsibility, Liability Responsibility, and Role Responsibility.

- Taking responsibility facilitates a learning environment. It allows you to identify what went wrong, adjust your strategy, and persevere.

- If you find taking responsibility challenging, start with small, manageable tasks. Owning the smaller tasks fully will set the stage for handling bigger challenges.

- When you make a mistake, own up to it **immediately**. Honesty is the cornerstone for responsibility.

- Taking responsibility is an ongoing process, not a one-time event. It takes time, patience, and a willingness to grow and change.

- Taking responsibility results in better-decision making and long-term success.

- The barrier to greatness is often the inability to sustain the effort and discipline needed.

- A lack of systems in place is one of the main culprits in organizations that have issues with employees, leaders, and team members not taking responsibility. With a lack of accountability mechanisms, it is easy for individuals to avoid responsibility.

- If you lack trust, you may find yourself trying to control a situation or other people in order to reduce the chance of getting hurt in the process. Learn to trust by taking the steps necessary and seek out a mentor or coach.

- The Trustworthy Titans are the silent hunters. They are the ones you don't even realize are hunting.

CHAPTER 10

The Application of the Global G.R.I.T. System™

*"If you can't describe what
you are doing as a process,
you don't know what you're doing."*

W. Edwards Deming

The application of the Global G.R.I.T. System™ can be used universally in both business and for personal use. For example, in business, if you have had a bad quarter, you can implement the Global G.R.I.T. System™ to G.R.I.T. Through it™. You aren't going to bounce back by doing what you've already done and simply changing one area doesn't always change the trajectory. You need a system. It starts by instilling the four pillars of "Get it done," "Reframe thinking," "Impact others," and "Take responsibility," along with adopting the process and creating the right environment. Then, once you identify your grit type through the Grit Type Indicator™, you have a system in which you can identify if you have the right people in the right seats or if you are missing critical aspects of the grit mentality within your team to bounce back from a bad quarter. You can apply this same principle to any type of adversity (outlined in Chapter 4), including but not limited to:

- **Resolve, manage, and avoid team conflict:** G.R.I.T. Through It™
- **Manage market volatility and economic downturns:** G.R.I.T. Through It™
- **Develop a culture of excellence through mergers and acquisitions:** G.R.I.T. Through It™
- **Gain, train, and retain top talent:** G.R.I.T Through It™
- **Performance through adversity:** G.R.I.T. Through It™
- **Recover quickly from funding and investment challenges:** G.R.I.T. Through It™
- **Performance through challenging times:** G.R.I.T. Through It™
- **Navigate political uncertainty:** G.R.I.T. Through It™
- **Navigate life after divorce:** G.R.I.T. Through It™
- **Life after losing a loved one:** G.R.I.T. Through It™
- **Life after college:** G.R.I.T. Through It™
- **PTSD and the aftermath:** G.R.I.T. Through It™

When the Global G.R.I.T. System™ and the Grit Type Indicator™ are used simultaneously, you will be able to identify where you as a company or an individual need to concentrate and pivot to ensure you have the right people around you (your culture of excellence). Then you will be able to create experiences not just for you, but for others to make an impact and become either the market leaders or innovators of your time. Furthermore, applying the Global G.R.I.T. System™ in your personal life will change the way you think, the way you behave, the skills you harness, and your environment. If you are really looking to make that next step in your life and aren't sure how to begin, you need to understand how to apply the Global G.R.I.T. System™ to not just yourself but for others around you.

PART 1:
Get it Done (G)

The Global Perspective

A "get it done" attitude is not confined to a specific culture or one particular area of the world. It is a state of mind—a mindset. A mindset that requires a system to achieve it. Apply the system and it can be accomplished globally. It is a part of our evolution and survival to have a sense of urgency, with each of us hardwired with this ability;[1] however, our instinct to use it is not automatic, and not genetically predetermined; instead, it is developed.[2] This proves that the "G" in the Global G.R.I.T. System™ can absolutely be developed and taught, we just have to master the tools to know how to tap into it. Our environment is more important in evolution than random mutation, meaning that our environment will determine whether we develop what we already have or lose it.[3] It is why the mentality of the grit you choose and the grit you don't is so essential to building up all areas of the Global G.R.I.T. System™. Can we choose our environment? Some say yes, others say no. In Chapter 2 I explained how I needed to change my environment and surround myself with a culture of excellence. I came to America. I changed my environment. I chose my own grit. Because of that, my "G" in the Global G.R.I.T. System™ strengthened, and I was able to pull from the "G" in the times I needed it the most, when grit chose me. It became a behavior, versus a skill.

Scheduling and organizing time is essential to master the "Get it done" mindset as highlighted in Chapter 6. Let's take a look back at what I said with regards to the Eisenhower Matrix. When we identify the tasks we need to complete and then organize them in a way that requires time management, it takes away the paralyzing feeling of needing to carry out many tasks at once, and giving up when we feel overwhelmed. It feels exhausting when we see a mountain we have to climb, but if we just look at it one section at a time, step by step, it doesn't seem so daunting. It's about prioritizing the tasks today that are going to get you a step closer to where you need to be tomorrow. The mountain represents the monumental tasks you may be facing. The peak seems far away and the path uncertain, generating those feelings of anxiety, concern, and apprehension. We don't just approach the mountain with no plan or strategy. If you do, you are likely to fail, give up, and be forced to turn around because of your lack of preparation. Instead, there is a system for how you attack such a task. Planning the route and studying the mountain's terrain to select the route to the summit, with markers for the "rest points," is the first objective. Followed by gearing up with food, water, a compass, clothing, and any other necessary resources needed for the task. Depending on the size of the mountain, you also need to set up a "base camp." This acts as a starting point and fallback location that creates a foundation from which you can operate. Climb to the first ascent the rest point on the map you identified when planning the route and identify this as a win. This is a significant achievement.

You may face adversity while climbing the mountain and you may have to adapt your route when faced with weather or other things out of your control. Additionally, it is important to celebrate other milestones you have reached along the route. This provides the motivation to keep going, because you have instilled the belief that you are achieving what you set out to perform when at the base of the mountain. Accomplishing smaller tasks builds momentum that allows you to achieve the bigger goal. Finally, taking time to reflect at the summit is an important part of the process. You can look back at the journey you have just managed, evaluate the process, and recognize your growth in areas you previously thought not possible.

Now relate this to a business goal, such as meeting an ambitious sales target for the year. The number may seem daunting and can trigger those feelings of uncertainty, but when you break the target down into manageable objectives, it can be highly achievable. When you divide the annual goal into quarterly, monthly, weekly, and even daily goals, it becomes less overwhelming. When you design a strategy to achieve the daily or weekly tasks needed to earn the goals, you start to believe that it is possible, which gives you motivation. This is the backbone of a "Get it Done" mindset. You need to start with a system. That could be understanding your environment (market demand and competition), identifying the sales target (quarterly, monthly, weekly), or identifying the resources needed to carry out the daily tasks necessary to achieve the weekly goal. Then create detailed plans and tactics for achieving each minor goal and put your plans into action, initiating the first steps toward your main objective while continually monitoring your progress and adapting your methods when needed. Be sure to celebrate when you meet a weekly, monthly, or quarterly goal. This will help you succeed. Use this momentum from your previous wins to tackle the remaining challenges and complete the remaining tasks. Finally, evaluate what worked and what didn't for future planning. Once you've achieved the larger goal, review the process to identify lessons and areas for improvement and ensure you have a plan in place to help with the improvement, such as coaching or a program for you and your team that will enhance performance. Each step toward meeting the sales target serves as a breakthrough, helping to make a daunting objective more attainable. This same principle can be applied to achieve the Get it Done mindset in the Global G.R.I.T. System™.

Challenges

Those who procrastinate may argue that they work better under pressure, and live in the "important and urgent" box of the Eisenhower Matrix. The answer to this is to create your own pressure to complete the tasks necessary to reach the goals you set before the tasks start to dictate to you and become unmanageable. Move the deadlines up for projects that need completing. This way you will slowly start to shift into the "important and not urgent" box and discover that you actually complete more goals as a result, because you understand and have reframed your thinking around procrastination. Goal-management ability underlies the genetic commonality between procrastination and impulsivity.[4] In other words, there are genetic predispositions to procrastination and impulsivity, showing a positive correlation. Additionally, procrastination may lead to an impulsive response when deadlines are fast approaching.[5] Thus, one of the strategies is to move the deadline up for those who have a genetic predisposition to procrastination. Work toward the deadline you set versus the deadline the organization sets. The environment you create determines whether or not the genetic predisposition comes out; therefore, the environment you surround yourself with plays a large part in the process you adopt and are able to maintain in the long run.[6]

It is important to note that "Go-getters" typically embrace stress versus trying to reduce it, which is why the other types of the Grit Type Indicator™ may find it challenging to understand the mindset of a "go-getter." Ultimately, the pressures of life within the environment you create affect your physiological systems, which induces the stress.[7] Consequently, when you master the ability to manage your stress, you master the ability to get things done without putting it off, landing you in the "important and not urgent" box.

Other reasons why some may find it difficult to get things done is that they are disinterested in the task. However, that particular task is one that may get you closer to your end goal in the long-term. Thus, it is important to categorize the tasks and draw a timeline of when tasks need to be completed by what date in order to hit each milestone, which gets you closer to the end goal. Look back at the analogy of the mountain. If you skip a step in that process, you are likely to fail at the end goal. It is no different when adopting the "G" in the Global G.R.I.T. System™. Sometimes we have to complete the tasks that have least appeal in order to reach the ones that have the most appeal. The tasks will still be there whether you decide to do them now or later, but procrastinating induces stress. This stress may lead to illness, disease, and long-term effects, physiologically as well as psychologically.[8]

Opportunities

Your social and physical surroundings significantly impact both the body and mind via the hormonal, automatic nervous, and immune systems.[9] This understanding isn't just a scientific observation, it's a blueprint for action, especially if you are in need of enhancing the "G" in the Global G.R.I.T. System™, aiming to become a "go-getter" with a "get it done" attitude. With that in mind, we can use that as an opportunity to create processes that align with the positive environment we create around us, allowing us to complete the tasks in the way that will enhance our performance and move us onto the next set of responsibilities. Surround yourself with others who are goal-oriented and supportive. Their energy is infectious and can give you the belief needed to achieve your goals. Additionally, being accountable to someone other than yourself can dramatically increase your chances of success. A positive reinforcement can stimulate the hormonal and neurological pathways that enhance performance.[10] This means a supportive social environment will also contribute to your success in achieving the "Get it Done" mentality.

Where you work, how you work, and the environment you create at work will significantly impact your mental state when completing tasks.[11] Create an environment that minimizes distractions and maximizes productivity. Following the five pillars that I outline in Chapter 3 will positively impact your hormonal and immune systems, which contributes to your energy levels needed to "Get it Done." Reducing physical stress such as your ergonomic work settings will allow your autonomic nervous system to focus on the tasks at hand.[12]

Creating processes is essential to adopt the "Get it Done" pillar of the Global G.R.I.T. System™, starting with prioritization by using the Eisenhower Matrix outlined in Chapter 6. Knowing what to focus on first will help ease the feelings of being overwhelmed. Time management is a behavior that can be learned in order to achieve the "Get it Done" element. Time-blocking is a great start to managing your time effectively and being disciplined by scheduling the time on your calendar to complete various tasks that need to be completed within a certain time frame. Regularly assessing the effectiveness of your processes and being willing to adapt will lead to a "Get it Done" mindset and the capability to take on new tasks. You have to be willing to consciously shape your social and physical environments in order to condition your body and mind with a "Get it Done" mindset, and that is where your culture of excellence comes in. Surround yourself with those who are the "G" in the Global G.R.I.T. System™ and you will learn how to hunt as a "go-getter" in the times you need it most. Those who are not task-orientated may find this pillar of grit most challenging, however through practice and techniques such as time-blocking, you will learn this skill over time. Consistency is key and you may need an accountability partner, such as a mentor or coach, to help you learn this skill to turn it into a behavior.

Real World Example

Take Michael Jordan as an example. Arguably the greatest basketball player of all time, he is the unequivocal example of a go-getter. He says, "I can accept failure, everyone fails at something. But I can't accept not trying".[13] In other words, failure is inevitable when we push ourselves past our comfort zone. But we learn from it, we get back up, and we try again. We just try a different way.

How do we achieve this? By committing to a small task. Once you complete it, move on to the next small task. This builds trust within yourself that you can do it, which creates the belief and the belief provides the motivation for you to continue. Your surroundings and environment play an important role in whether you commit to getting something complete or not. Remember to choose your culture of excellence and if you are not surrounded by "go-getters" and need to enhance this area of your grit, then surround yourself with "go-getters," watch them, study them, learn from them, hunt with them. This can include fellow team members, friends, mentors, coaches, and leaders.

PART 2:
Reframe Thinking (R)

The Global Perspective

Our reactions to situations are often conditioned by our cultural, social, and personal experiences.[14] The ability to reframe one's mindset is not just a personal advantage, it's a global necessity. Whether you are a leader in New York City or a community organizer in a small village, the challenges of today's world demand a shift in perspective. Understanding multiple viewpoints is essential in a global society and having an understanding of different cultures and environments is critical. How you view a situation may not be the same as a team member or friend, owing to their upbringing, experience, and societal values. We have to be aware of these influences and reframe how we approach a situation when working in a diverse culture. In a world that's increasingly interconnected and complex, reframing how we perceive adversity is not just beneficial, it's essential. Instead of viewing a problem as a stress-inducing issue, view it as a challenge that offers an opportunity for personal and collective growth. One way to do this is by removing yourself from the situation and looking at the situation objectively. Look at the facts and be aware of your feelings. The two may differ.

The emotional part of our brain (the limbic system) is the oldest part of our brain.[15] Thus, we have to work harder for the logic to override the emotions in many cases. Remember, we are programmed with a negativity bias as part of our survival instinct from thousands of years ago.[16] When we are aware of this we are able to catch our thoughts and reprogram what we tell ourselves about the situation so we can reframe it in a positive light. Even with severe adversity, this is possible. When my son, Jack, passed away, I couldn't see the positive at all. I still don't and never will see my son passing as a positive. But, what I have done is reframed how I thought about his passing. Rather than thinking he was taken from me, I think he was given to me, even if for a short while. For that I am eternally grateful, because he's impacted not just my life, but millions of others, including yours, as I most likely wouldn't have created and developed the Global G.R.I.T. System™ without his passing and my experiencing severe adversity.

Whether in the workplace or personally, viewing challenges as opportunities rather than as negative obstacles can be the difference between stagnation and innovation. In essence, how we frame these challenges determines not only our immediate response but also sets the stage for long-term success or failure. By embracing challenges as catalysts for improvement, we open the door to new solutions, enhanced thinking, control of emotions, greater resilience, and ultimately, a more fulfilling and impactful life and career.

Challenges

Our past experiences and future expectations shape our moment-to-moment thoughts as well as our deeper belief systems.[17] These foundational assumptions often go unnoticed but can be the source of significant stress in our lives, both at home and in the workplace. Awareness of these ingrained beliefs, especially when you notice recurring negative thought patterns during challenging situations, is essential to master the reframe thinking pillar of the Global G.R.I.T. System™. Persistent cycles of negative thinking can contribute to ongoing depression, which has been linked to a reduction in the size of key brain regions like the hippocampus and prefrontal cortex.[18] This implies that long-term negative thinking associated with emotional struggles can have tangible, detrimental effects on brain health and cognitive function.

Challenges associated with mastering the "Reframe thinking" pillar of the Global G.R.I.T. System™ includes being able to be self-aware and recognizing you have these ingrained beliefs in the first place. This requires you to be honest with yourself. Perhaps you may need to discuss with a mentor or coach to identify your belief patterns in this area. Additionally, even if you are self-aware of these ingrained beliefs, confronting those beliefs may pose a challenge due to the emotional discomfort associated with it, particularly if these assumptions have guided you throughout your life to date. External influences are also a challenge as your culture, family, and friends may reinforce these deep-seated beliefs. Also, immediate gratification versus the long-term benefit is also a challenge for many who have not harnessed the behavior of the "R" in the Global G.R.I.T. System™. The long-term benefits may be immense but if that causes discomfort in the short-term, this can cause a roadblock to being able to master the skills needed to create the behavior necessary to adopt "Reframe thinking" as part of your grit. If your work environment resists change, this too can pose a problem. Providing evidence as to why change is necessary will be advantageous for your position. Show your employer or employees why you need to be in an environment that will allow you the opportunity to adopt such a skill set and behavior.

Opportunities

The brain acts as the central hub for regulating stress and adapting to challenges.[19] By changing our perception of "stress" from a burden to simply a neutral condition, we can generate new behavioral responses. To achieve this, we need to establish new patterns of behavior, like the five pillars explored in Chapter 3. This empowers us to reframe our thinking when confronted with situations that we might have previously considered threatening. Understanding that there are alternative thought patterns, contrary to our natural instincts, enables us to modify the wiring of our brains. This shift affects our physiological reactions, leading either to successful adaptation or, if not managed well, to allostasis that may result in illness.[20]

Acknowledging the situation and your initial emotional response is the first step to recognizing and being aware of how you may be able to reframe your thinking and thus your reaction. This allows you to brainstorm possible solutions, which also allows you to take a step back from being "in" the situation and view it as though you are a "third" person. When you identify opportunities instead of only seeing the negative you will be able to focus on actionable steps you can take to help change your perspective, and the beliefs of others, about the situation. It will provide a sense of control over your own emotions, reactions, and thoughts, which will reduce stress and champion a proactive attitude.[21] Identifying thought distortions will allow you to reframe how you think about the situation and change the negative distortion to a positive reinforcement that will alter your physical reaction when saying the words out loud.[22] Another approach is to imagine pouring a huge cauldron of iced water over a raging fire. This allows you to take control of your immediate response and calm your thoughts surrounding a situation and instead gain control of the immediate negative thoughts or emotionally charged reaction to a situation.

Using our "wise mind"[23] to become aware of our automatic thoughts and the emotions they trigger is an opportunity to practice the consciousness of our thoughts. This takes time and practice with practical applications, and is best practiced via a coach for both individual and team settings. Practicing smaller, less-emotionally charged issues to build confidence in this area is a great start before you move on to more significant challenges. By mastering the "reframe thinking" element of the Global G.R.I.T. System™ you not only improve your capacity to manage adversity, but also build a pillar of the grit mindset that is a cornerstone for leadership, not just in the workplace but outside of it, both locally and on a global scale.

Real World Example

Chris Gardner, whose life story inspired the movie *The Pursuit of Happyness* (2016), faced incredible challenges, including homelessness, sleeping in a public restroom, single fatherhood, and no connections or education in the finance industry. However, he became a multi-millionaire stockbroker. How did he do it? Well, what sets Chris Gardner apart is his ability to reframe adversity into opportunity. He didn't view himself as a victim, he saw himself as the victor. He reframed his reality and took control of his thoughts to tell himself that he had the power to change his own destiny.[24] When he faced obstacles such as a lack of education and experience, he found a way around it and became committed to learning from every single setback he had. As a result of his reframe thinking ability he went from being homeless with zero industry knowledge, to owning his own brokerage firm, all by reframing his circumstances. He clearly demonstrates how the "R" in the Global G.R.I.T. System™ can be put into practice with adversity serving as the beginning of a new chapter filled with opportunities for growth, rather than the end of the story.

What does this teach us? It teaches us that once you have acknowledged the situation and your initial emotional responses to it, you can objectively evaluate the challenge and brainstorm solutions either individually, or as a team. Once you have identified the problem as an opportunity, you can now focus on the actionable steps you can take to solve it, giving you back control of your own thoughts and thus behavior associated with those thoughts. Whether you are dealing with conflict at work, job loss, personal failure, grief, trauma, or any other problems that can cause stress, reframing how you think will teach you how to hunt in times when you need a more methodical, calm approach to be able to hunt successfully. This will allow you time to learn the skill set necessary to turn into a behavior and study other "reframers" to learn real-life examples of how they have turned adversity into an advantage.

PART 3:
Impact Others (I)

The Global Perspective

Inspiration is the spark that fuels individuals to initiate innovation and take their ideas from concept to completion[25] and is critical when you are committed to driving transformative change in individuals, teams, companies, organizations, and industries worldwide. It creates immense impact for others. With that in mind, we are in a world that's increasingly interconnected, and the scope of our actions and decisions often reaches beyond local or even national boundaries. Our decisions and choices have ripple effects that go way beyond our local community.

As we are in a globally connected world, when you impact others positively through your actions, behavior, and leadership, you are laying the foundation for an environment and creating a setting where everyone can win on your team. What truly inspires others is showing how you are not self-serving, but rather how you put your team's needs first. Why? Because whatever culture you create among your team is the same culture your clients and community are experiencing from your organization. Real innovation solves problems and you can't solve problems effectively without understanding the people experiencing them. A focus on others naturally drives you toward solutions that make a meaningful difference. Positive, lasting change is change that benefits everyone involved while building trust, loyalty, and credibility. Additionally, when you don't make it about you but you make it about others, that's when true legacies are built. Not from your individual success story, but through the stories of success with the waves of people you have helped elevate and inspire, whose own stories of grit will continue to inspire for many years. So don't make it about you. To drive real change in others, in your team, in your organization and outside of it, you need to develop the "I" in the Global G.R.I.T. System™ that can face challenges, impact others, and inspire many to harness the innovation from within that creates the real change in teams, culture, companies, organizations, and industries.

Impacting others and acts of generosity are shown to boost happiness, creating a cycle that further encourages generous actions.[26] As a result, a focus on others naturally drives you toward solutions that make a meaningful difference. Research offers both behavioral and neural proof that there's a connection between being generous and feeling "happy." These findings indicate that to truly gain happiness through acts of generosity, and impacting others, areas of the brain related to empathy and social understanding must override self-centered motives in regions tied to rewards.[27]

Challenges

For anyone committed to making a real impact for others, there are challenges that can serve as barriers. Shifting the focus from "me" to "we" is a vital step in overcoming these and truly inspiring change. When an individual has been focused on themselves, they may find the shift to focus on others challenging, which makes it harder to understand the collective needs and problems that require solving. As a leader, if you do not impact others and inspire, you will find that your team members are less likely to trust you than if you were to show genuine concern for others and make it about them, not about you. Why is this important? Because without loyalty and trust, you don't have a team. The focus should be on building the relationships with your team members to be able to impact them in an inspirational way so they have an environment where they can be creative and innovate.

Furthermore, there may well be reduced collaboration with others not wanting to form part of a "team" if the "team" setting is more individualistic. This directly impacts motivation in others, with engagement being affected along with productivity levels being damaged, leading to higher turnover rates. Of course, without the ability to impact others, there will be a lack of innovation among the team and thus the organization. This was highlighted in Chapter 8 as the foundation for long-term success to thrive in any industry. This leads to missed opportunities for growth and a reduction in diverse skills with difficulty adapting to new situations, limiting one's own effectiveness, and grit. Additionally, people talk. If you are focused on yourself, and do not have a mindset of impacting others, this may very well limit opportunities for partnerships, promotions, or new roles within your organization.

Opportunities

Making a meaningful difference in the lives of others not only fuels personal development but also harvests an environment where innovation can thrive. When you focus on impacting others, you are empowering them to bring their A-game. You are unlocking their hidden potential and you may discover hidden potential among team members you didn't know existed. They could emerge as the innovators within your team. The opportunity to build a culture of excellence exists when you impact others. When you show what's possible through your inspiration to others, you will find that others are more willing to delve outside of their comfort zone and create an environment where innovative ideas can flourish. This in turn will build synergy among the team, as impacting others positively encourages teamwork.[28] This may lead to new perspectives and solutions that previously may not have been thought possible. Impacting others through inspiring them to innovate accelerates problem-solving[29] and paves the way for quicker, more effective solutions.

The opportunity to build meaningful, deep relationships with others prevails when impacting others is a focus. It opens the door to potential collaborations, long-term partnerships and alliances, all of which can be invaluable for future innovation. Consequently, a leader who impacts others is likely to attract a wider network of professionals, thinkers, and doers (in fact, all four pillars of the Global G.R.I.T. System™). These connections and the network you build through impacting others can serve as incubators for fresh ideas and initiatives.

An important point to take away from impacting others is the fact that employees and team members are often more engaged when they feel that their work is impactful. When they are more engaged they contribute the most to innovative projects.[30]

It is important to remember that in a world where we are interconnected, a locally successful innovation can quickly become a global phenomenon. Leaders who focus on impacting others have the chance to make a difference on a much larger scale, not just within their team or organization, but across the industry.

Real World Example

Steve Jobs serves as an ultimate example of a leader who profoundly impacted others and spurred innovation as a result. He focused on inspiring his team to think differently and break the status quo; in the process, he created his "culture of excellence." Steve Jobs had a unique ability to inspire his team to achieve what seemed impossible.[31] He set incredibly high expectations, which initially seemed unattainable, but he had the impact and vision to help people believe that they could achieve these advanced goals. His impact set a standard for the tech industry worldwide, inspiring global innovation.

What does Steve Jobs teach us by impacting others? His ability to impact and inspire his team to push boundaries and strive for excellence was a guiding light for others. He led by example and aimed to revolutionize entire industries, encouraging a culture of disruptive innovation. By empowering his team with resources and creative freedom, he laid the groundwork for a culture where groundbreaking ideas could thrive. Steve Jobs also demonstrated the dual scope of impactful leadership, having both local and global reach. Authenticity was his hallmark and he was unafraid to be himself, even when it wasn't popular.[32] This teaches us the importance of authenticity in leadership. Genuine interactions can inspire loyalty and lead to greater impact. His resilience in the face of adversity was legendary, and the legacy he left behind transcends products and profits. His work teaches us that by impacting others through inspiration, leaders can create an environment where innovation flourishes, leaving a lasting impact on people, teams, organizations, and industries worldwide.

Empower your team through impacting them in a positive way. By giving your team the resources and freedom to do their best work, you empower them to be creative and thus innovative with their approach. In doing so, you create a ripple effect not just in your company, but in your industry.

Being the innovators and change makers will raise the bar and set the standard.

Leaders who focus on helping others "hunt" will actively seek out avenues to make a meaningful difference. They are not just focused on their own success, they aim to elevate everyone around them. They are relentless in their pursuit of excellence and are always on the hunt for ways to empower their teams.

PART 4:
Take Responsibility (T)

The Global Perspective

Taking responsibility as a leader is absolutely essential, not just for individual growth but for shaping the collective ethos of a team. When you, as a leader, make it a point to take responsibility for your actions, decisions, and even your mistakes, you set a powerful example for your team to follow.

Primarily, it builds trust. Team members are more likely to trust a leader who takes responsibility for their decisions and is accountable for the results. Trust is the base upon which strong, meaningful, lasting relationships are built. It also stimulates loyalty. When you take responsibility, you show that you're committed to integrity and ethical conduct. This naturally inspires loyalty among your team members, because they see you as a leader who stands by your values. As a result, your team will feel a greater sense of ownership over their tasks as your behavior has a ripple effect, and thus will naturally boost productivity as your team will become more focused and committed to achieving long-term goals. By taking responsibility, you show your team that every action has a consequence, whether good or bad, and that it matters.[33] This sense of significance can be contagious, enhancing engagement levels within the team and even influencing behavior beyond the workplace. This ripple effect can positively impact the local community and the client experience.[34]

As a leader, your approach to taking responsibility doesn't just affect you. It becomes part of the DNA of your team, shaping how they interact with each other, which impacts the "I" in the Global G.R.I.T. System™. It also impacts how they innovate and influence each other. Over time, this creates a culture of accountability that will positively impact the overall performance of your team and prepare them to take on challenges that they might not have faced previously with the same vigor. In essence, by taking responsibility, you're not just creating a culture of accountability, you are shaping future leaders.

Challenges

The challenges that some may face with taking responsibility include the fear of consequence and what might happen if they admit a mistake or take the fall for the team, worrying that it could put their position within the organization at risk.[35] Ego comes into play too. Acknowledging mistakes can feel like a blow to their ego and self-image.[36] A lack of awareness due to the leader failing to recognize that a problem exists or that they have made a mistake may prevent them from taking responsibility. Additionally, leaders who are more focused on short-term goals with immediate results may opt for quick fixes versus taking the time to accept responsibility and create long-term solutions.[37] Subsequently, a leader may not want to admit a mistake owing to social pressure and the desire of wanting a flawless image.[38] Some leaders may lack the skill needed to navigate the complexities of human behavior and emotions and have a low EQ, which makes taking responsibility daunting for them.[39]

Facing these challenges head-on is a must for any leader looking to create a culture of accountability and integrity. It sets a powerful example for your team, enhancing trust, loyalty, and ultimately, productivity.

Opportunities

Taking responsibility boosts trust among your team, lays the groundwork for a high-engagement culture, and catalyzes innovation.[40] Your team looks to you to set the standard, and when you embody responsibility, you set the stage for a cohesive, motivated, and loyal workforce. This not only harnesses professional growth for both you and your team but also gives your entire organization a strategic advantage in adapting to market changes and seizing new opportunities.

The impact of responsible leadership isn't just confined to your immediate environment. Your actions set a global example, influencing industry standards and even shaping societal norms.[41] Taking responsibility is a long-term strategy that prepares you, those around you, and your organization for sustained long-term success. It enhances your reputation and attracts and retains top talent while opening doors to new opportunities. Ultimately, taking responsibility as a leader is an invaluable asset for the entire company. It has a ripple effect across teams within the organization and creates a culture of accountability.

What can we learn from this? Taking responsibility is not a burden, it is an opportunity for personal, team, and organizational development, which lays the foundation for a leadership style that others can mirror, both within the immediate circle and on a larger scale across the organization.

Real World Example

Abraham Lincoln, the 16th President of the United States, stands as a timeless example of a leader who exhibited tremendous responsibility and trustworthiness. At a pivotal time in American history, Lincoln navigated the nation through its most severe crisis: the Civil War. His leadership wasn't about shifting responsibility; he assumed full ownership for the country's actions, including both victories and failures on the battlefield and the home front.[42]

One example that stands out is Lincoln's handling of the Battle of Gettysburg. Although the Union won, the victory came at a high cost, with thousands of casualties. Lincoln didn't cast blame on his generals or soldiers. Instead, he took the opportunity to reflect on the broader significance of the war and the sacrifices made, culminating in the Gettysburg Address.[43] This poignant speech did more than commemorate a battle, it clarified the moral underpinnings of the war and redefined the conflict as a struggle for equality. In doing so, Lincoln fortified public trust not only in him but also in the American system of governance. He understood that for a nation to heal and move forward, its leader must assume ultimate responsibility, providing a moral and ethical compass for its citizens. His commitment to his principles and his open acknowledgment of the weight of his decisions made him a "Trustworthy Titan." Lincoln's example illuminates the profound impact that a responsible leader can have, setting a standard that echoes through time.

"Trustworthy Titans" are leaders who combine strategic vision, skill, and ethical integrity to excel in their fields and earn the respect and loyalty of their team members. Much like skilled hunters, these leaders are strategically astute, well-prepared, and highly adaptable. They maintain a deep understanding of market dynamics, continually invest in personal and team development, and have the agility to pivot when faced with new challenges or opportunities. Beyond just targeting short-term gains, they focus on creating an environment that benefits the entire team. The trust they earn comes from their commitment to ethical behavior and transparent communication, making them not just successful but also models of integrity and authenticity. In essence, they "hunt" for opportunities, for talent, and for authenticity in a manner that creates trust while building a legacy, contributing to sustainable growth.

PART 5:
Company Examples of Applying the Global G.R.I.T. System™

Apple

In the late 1990s Apple was teetering on the edge of bankruptcy, posting a staggering loss of 1.04 billion dollars. However, they orchestrated a miraculous turnaround, generating a profit of 309 million dollars within just a year.[44] Recognizing the need for radical change, the company reframed their thinking and streamlined its focus to core products: two desktops and two portables, each tailored for either professionals or consumers. This wasn't just a business pivot, it was a cultural overhaul. Inspired by Steve Jobs' visionary leadership, the Apple team was energized to rethink their strategies and reignite the company's prospects. They embodied the core tenets of the Global G.R.I.T. System™, including a "get-it-done" approach. Instead of viewing Microsoft as a fierce competitor, they reframed their perspective, seeing an opportunity for partnership and co-existence in the tech industry.[45] Even when faced with setbacks, like the G4 cube fiasco in 2000, when they had their least profitable quarter in three years,[46] Apple didn't back down. They embraced failure as part of the innovation process, took responsibility, and weren't afraid to take risks. Continually launching fresh, groundbreaking products and attracting diverse talent, Apple cultivated a system of inspiration and action. They moved decisively, without hesitation, cementing their position as a tech titan. As of August 2023, this unstoppable momentum has vaulted Apple to a market cap of nearly 2.8 trillion dollars, outpacing Microsoft's 2.4 trillion dollar cap.[47] This remarkable achievement can be credited to the way Steve Jobs led the company when he returned as CEO and to Apple's diverse team; a powerhouse combo of go-getters, reframers, innovators, and trustworthy titans.

Airbnb

Airbnb's journey exemplifies the embodiment of the Global G.R.I.T. System™. When the company's founders were struggling to pay rent, they took initiative and designed a website to rent out their loft as a bed and breakfast during a major conference.[48] This move demonstrated their "go-getter" attitude, capitalizing on existing resources to create new opportunities. They disrupted the traditional hotel industry by reframing the way people think about travel accommodations. They didn't see the challenge as a zero-sum competition with established hotels; instead, they envisioned a global community of hosts and travelers enriching each other's lives. From creating a new insurance policy to protect hosts to implementing machine-learning algorithms for smarter pricing and matchmaking, Airbnb has been a hub of innovation. They've continuously adapted their services to meet the evolving needs of both hosts and guests. The foundation of Airbnb's model relies on trust. By creating robust verification processes, encouraging open reviews, and establishing a responsive customer service team, they've built a marketplace that thrives on mutual respect and accountability. By internalizing these four pillars, Airbnb has not only survived but thrived, transforming from a small startup into a global powerhouse. The trajectory of Airbnb isn't just a success story, it's an ode to a remarkable team that lives and breathes the core tenets of the Global G.R.I.T. System™. Comprising go-getters who act decisively on opportunities, reframers who have rethought the traditional lodging experience, innovators continually revamping features for optimal user satisfaction, and trustworthy titans who've laid a foundation of unshakable trust, Airbnb's team has been a beacon of resilience and adaptability. This team, deeply entrenched in the qualities of grit outlined in the Global G.R.I.T. System™, has become the lifeblood of Airbnb's mission and vision. Their commitment to these principles has elevated Airbnb from a fledgling startup into a global beast in the hospitality industry, redefining what it means to explore and travel.

The Global G.R.I.T. System™ Applied:
Confront, Overcome, and Transcend

The true power of the Global G.R.I.T. System™ is its universal applicability, not just as a business methodology but as a life philosophy. When you incorporate the principles of the Global G.R.I.T. System™ into your ethos, you're not just surviving adversity, you're learning how to thrive through it. Whether you're navigating the uncertain waters of a volatile marketplace, mitigating team conflicts, or dealing with personal struggles such as PTSD or the loss of a loved one, the Global G.R.I.T. System™ offers a structured approach to confront, overcome, and transcend.

So, don't just go through life—G.R.I.T. Through It™. Understand that the path to transformative impact, whether as an individual or as a market leader, doesn't lie in avoiding difficulties, but in facing them head-on with resolve, perspective, responsibility, and a commitment to positive impact. If you're committed to making a change but unsure where to start, understand that the answer isn't "out there"—it's within you. And it begins the moment you decide to apply the Global G.R.I.T. System™ to your life and work. Harness the power of the Global G.R.I.T. System™ and watch how it not only changes you but sets off a ripple effect, inspiring those around you to aim higher, reach further, and live fuller.

The Global G.R.I.T. System™ is not just an attribute, it's a movement with the power to ignite transformative change across industries and lives.

So let's start that movement.

Now.

*"Systems run the business,
people run the systems."*

Michael Gerber

10 Key Leadership Lessons From This Chapter:

- Prioritize the tasks today that are going to get you a step closer to where you need to be tomorrow.

- The environment you surround yourself with plays a large part in the process you adopt and are able to stay consistent with in the long term.

- We have to complete the tasks that have least appeal in order to reach the ones that have the most appeal.

- Surround yourself with others who are goal-oriented and supportive. Their energy is infectious and can give you the belief you need to achieve your goals.

- Understanding multiple viewpoints is essential. How you view a situation may not be the same as others, owing to upbringing, experience, and societal values. Be aware of the influences and reframe how you approach a situation when working in a diverse culture.

- The ability to change our perception of "stress" from a burden to a neutral condition will generate new behavioral responses.

- Reframing how you think will teach you how to hunt.

- Real innovation solves problems and you can't solve problems effectively without understanding the people experiencing them.

- By taking responsibility, you're not just creating a culture of accountability, you are shaping future leaders.

- If you're committed to making a change but unsure where to start, understand that the answer isn't "out there"—it's within **you**.

CHAPTER 11

Commissioning the Global G.R.I.T. System™

"A system isn't just a roadmap to discipline—it's the key to unlocking the untapped potential that turns quitters into conquerors."

Lara Jones

Transforming Potential Into Performance

By this point in the book you should understand the pillars and terminology of the Global G.R.I.T. System™, grasping its core tenets deeply. You know that "Get it Done" isn't merely a tagline, it's a call to action. "Reframe Thinking" has likely already started to reshape your perspective on challenges, turning them into opportunities. You understand the immense value of "Impacting Others" and how that ripple effect can catalyze monumental change. And let's not forget the gravity of "Taking Responsibility," it's the foundation that makes everything else possible.

You've also learned the different "grit types" within the Global G.R.I.T. System™—the "Go-Getters" who kick down doors and who are relentless in their pursuit; the "Reframers" who change the game and look at everything differently, being able to turn negative situations into opportunities; the "Innovators" who bring a flair of originality and inspire others around them to achieve greatness; and the "Trustworthy Titans" who cement the foundation of any successful venture. All of which are identified through the "Grit Type Indicator™. Beyond that, you've been introduced to the specific process that helps you adopt the Global G.R.I.T. System™ in a realistic and applicable manner that will ensure long-term success.

Now comes the real work: turning principles into practice. Adopting the Global G.R.I.T. System™ isn't merely about understanding its four cornerstone elements. It's about committing to a deliberate process that maximizes the potential of every individual within your organization.

This chapter serves as your blueprint for commissioning the Global G.R.I.T. System™ into actionable plans that yield tangible results. Get ready to turn theory into transformative action.

SECTION 1:
Planning Phase—Know Your Starting Point

Before you can implement the process, you need to assess where you, your team, and your organization stand.

- **Personal Assessment:** Are you a go-getter? How do you currently reframe thinking, impacting others, and taking responsibility? How do you measure any of these attributes? How do you combine them together? Where are you most dominant, and where are your weaker points? It's essential to understand this. The Grit Type Indicator™ is designed to do all of that and more.

- **Organizational Audit:** Survey the existing culture, challenges, opportunities, and implement the Grit Type Indicator™ for the entire workforce. Identify the divisions in your company that require a specific type of grit based on the four pillars of the Global G.R.I.T. System™. Identify if you need additional grit types or need a shift around to leverage the dominant traits of people's strengths to increase engagement and ensure that team members are in alignment with not just your company's purpose but their own, individual purpose.

- **Objectives Setting:** Clearly define what you hope to achieve with the Global G.R.I.T. System™, both as a leader and within the company.

SECTION 2:
Implementation Phase

Implementing the Global G.R.I.T. System™ isn't about cherry-picking elements that fit conveniently into your current structure, it's about embracing the Global G.R.I.T. System™ as an interconnected framework. Each component—Get it Done, Reframe Thinking, Impact Others, and Take Responsibility—is like a gear in a well-oiled machine. They need to mesh seamlessly for the system to function at its highest capacity.

Example:

- **Get it Done:** Drives the action, but without the other elements it might be action without purpose.
- **Reframe Thinking:** Fuels innovation, but needs the grounding of responsibility and the forward motion of a "get it done" attitude otherwise action may not prevail.
- **Impact Others:** Adds the human touch, giving purpose and meaning to the tasks at hand. However, without reframing thinking the impact might be limited to conventional methods.
- **Take Responsibility:** Acts as the ethical compass, ensuring that the action taken and impact made align with core values and integrity. Without the get it done attitude, ethical intentions may never translate into actionable results.

In essence, each element complements and amplifies the others. Commissioning the Global G.R.I.T. System™ is about recognizing that grit—whether in leaders, team members, or entire organizations—comes from the alchemy of these four elements working in harmony. It's not a menu to choose from, it's a recipe to follow.

Understanding the Process

The process breakdown outlines the systematic approach needed to fully implement the Global G.R.I.T. System™ within any type of organizational structure:

- **Create Awareness:** By creating awareness of the Global G.R.I.T. System™ you discover appreciation and understanding of what it does and how it will benefit the individuals participating in the system. Understanding is the foundation upon which action is built.
- **Tailored Learning Environments:** Providing settings that cater to all three learning behavior styles—practical, auditory, and visual—ensures that everyone has the autonomy and the tools they need to grasp the system's principles.
- **Developing Belief:** Contrary to popular perception, grit isn't a trait you either have or don't. The process I have identified and created,

lived by me and backed by research, instills the belief that grit can be developed, fueling the motivation to harvest all its elements.

- **Cognitive Influence:** This motivation acts as a catalyst, triggering changes in cognition. As cognition is influenced, so are the brain's processes and patterns, paving the way for a growth mindset.
- **Growth Mindset:** When we influence our cognition we are rewiring our brain patterns, which leads to a positive attitude to unlock a growth mindset. With a growth mindset, the possibilities are endless. It is essential to learn how to cultivate a growth mindset to achieve the next step.
- **Adoption of the Global G.R.I.T. System™:** Adoption of the Global G.R.I.T. System™ is achieved, owing to our cognition being open to learning, and more importantly, applying the elements of the Global G.R.I.T. System™.

Applying the Global G.R.I.T. System™ is a symbiotic process that demands the engagement of each part to function as a whole. It's not a buffet of options, it's an evolving blueprint tailored to the distinct needs of your organization and team.

Execution Steps

1. **Training and Development:** Initiate a Global G.R.I.T. System™ workshop, event, or program.
2. **Early Adoption:** Start with one department or project or multiple department heads going through the training together. This creates trust and loyalty.
3. **Full Implementation:** Roll it out across the board to create your "culture of excellence" and develop grit in every single team member.

Assembling Your "Grit Team"

No one succeeds alone. Who are your dominant go-getters, reframers, innovators, and trustworthy titans? Achieving success is a team effort that hinges on identifying and leveraging the unique talents within your group. You'll need your dominant grit types in each area:

go-getters who drive initiatives forward, reframers who turn challenges into opportunities, innovators who bring fresh solutions, and trustworthy titans who uphold the team's integrity. Knowing what to look for in your team members is only half the battle; the real magic happens when you strategically assemble these diverse individuals into a cohesive and functional unit, optimized to meet the multifaceted demands of today's fast-paced environment. Elevating the development process to not only teach but also instill the behaviors of each grit type transforms individuals into masters of all four pillars of grit. This profound shift doesn't just revolutionize your leadership, it elevates the entire organization and even sets new standards for the industry.

The key to a high-performing team lies in not only identifying the right talent, specifically pinpointing go-getters, reframers, innovators, and trustworthy titans, but also in strategically assembling these individuals into a cohesive, well-functioning unit.

Imagine a team where every member has been empowered by the Global G.R.I.T. System™ program to discern when to channel specific aspects of their developed grit. Whether it's showcasing a go-getter's drive or a reframer's ingenuity, they're not just making choices—they're executing strategies. This mastery allows them to deftly apply these facets of grit in diverse real-world scenarios, both professionally and personally. Far more than just honing skills, they're cultivating transformative behaviors that enrich their entire lives.

Optimal Team Structure: How to Assemble These Individuals Into a Functioning Unit

- **Strategic Placement:** Position your dominant Go-Getters in roles that require quick decision making and immediate action. They are your front-liners who can drive projects forward.
- **Idea Incubation:** Place your dominant Reframers in planning and strategy roles. They will help the team navigate through challenges by encouraging different viewpoints and solutions.
- **Solution Engineering:** Dominant Innovators fit best in roles that require creative problem-solving. They can work in research and

development, product development, marketing, or any other areas that require fresh perspectives.

- **Governance and Oversight:** Dominant Trustworthy Titans should be in positions that involve compliance, quality assurance, or roles that require high levels of trust and reliability.

By intentionally assembling a team that encapsulates the grit elements you're not just setting up a group of individuals, you're crafting a dynamic, versatile unit that is more than capable of rising to the challenges ahead. The synergy of these unique talents will create a culture of excellence, enhance productivity, and elevate the collective capabilities of your organization.

SECTION 3:
Sustaining and Review Phase

This is a crucial component in the lifecycle of commissioning the Global G.R.I.T. System™. After initial rollout and training, it's tempting to believe the work is done. However, the real magic lies in sustaining these principles and conducting ongoing evaluations. This phase involves regular assessments to see how well the system is being integrated into daily operations and culture. The review process allows you to identify areas of grit improvement within yourself, your team, and your organization, thereby transforming your approach from static to dynamic. Here, you adapt and fine-tune your strategy to meet the evolving challenges and needs of your team and the broader organization from a grit perspective. After all, the Global G.R.I.T. System™ isn't just a one-off initiative, it's a long-term commitment to excellence.

Tailoring the Global G.R.I.T. System™ for You

Your goals will shape how the Global G.R.I.T. System™ is deployed. They are the compass that directs the ship. Your goals will determine the path you'll take and the strategies you'll employ. This is especially true when implementing the Global G.R.I.T. System™. Whether you're seeking to revolutionize an industry, create team unity, or forge stronger client relationships, the way you deploy the Global G.R.I.T. System™ will vary to meet those unique objectives. The beauty of the Global G.R.I.T. System™ lies in its flexibility–it's a tool that can be customized. So as you embark on your journey, remember that aligning the Global G.R.I.T. System™ with your specific goals is not just an option, it's essential for success.

Monitoring and Adjusting

In a constantly evolving business landscape, the Global G.R.I.T. System™ isn't just adaptable- it's indispensable. Ongoing training isn't merely beneficial, it's non-negotiable. For new recruits, seasoned team members, leaders, individuals, and aspiring leaders, the system serves as an invaluable barometer of grit, shaping not just performance but team dynamics, culture, and even talent acquisition and retention strategies. For seasoned team members, refresher courses are essential, not optional. They ensure that grit levels in all four pillars are not just maintained, but continually elevated. The Global G.R.I.T. System™ isn't just a tool for development, it's a dynamic framework for sustained excellence.

Reviewing the Global G.R.I.T. System™

By meticulously planning, implementing, sustaining, and reviewing the Global G.R.I.T. System™, you ensure it's effectively embedded in the organization's DNA. This is incredibly important as it will create the belief in others, which is the catalyst for motivation, which in turn influences cognition and alters brain patterns to be able to cultivate the growth mindset and adopt the Global G.R.I.T. System™. This is not just a one-off event but a cultural shift that will drive long-term performance and resilience.

SECTION 4:
Systematic Approach to Grit

Resilience isn't a static quality, it evolves through our engagement with our environment and matures throughout our developmental journey.[1] The implication is clear: the more we actively seek to cultivate grit, the better equipped we are when life's challenges inevitably come knocking.

Supported by research that contends resilience is not a trait held by a select few but a capacity we all possess,[2] the Global G.R.I.T. System™ serves as a comprehensive platform and system for grit development. From its foundational to its actionable processes and diagnostic tools, this system is a comprehensive solution for identifying, developing, strengthening, and applying grit, no matter the circumstance. It empowers you to lean into the most effective form of grit for each specific situation and ensures that team members are aligned with roles that best suit their own unique brand of grit. When we make a conscious choice to cultivate grit or find ourselves chosen by circumstances that require it, our life priorities undergo a seismic shift. This shift incites a transformative cognitive process that champions a growth mindset, thereby allowing for the effective application of the Global G.R.I.T. System™ in facing life's challenges.

Leading with Grit

To lead with grit is to lead with fortitude. To lead with the Global G.R.I.T. System™ is to lead with groundbreaking innovation that will make you a lion among wildebeest. Remember, hunting alone you might go fast but will only go so far. Hunting together means you will hunt for longer and have more wins. To employ a cooperative hunting strategy, together as a team or group, you must pull from each other's strengths to ambush your prey. Lions and lionesses rely on teamwork, with some members of the pride working together to encircle and bring down their chosen target while others provide support or guard against potential escape of their prey. Your team is your pride of lions. If you are not hunting together, you are at risk of falling as a group and being hunted. Focus on your strengths, be aware of your weaknesses, and pull from each other to create a power team and birth your "culture of excellence".

It is not enough to just know your dominant grit type. Simply identifying your dominant grit type offers only a partial view of your capabilities. You need to master all four pillars of grit in the Global G.R.I.T. System™ to truly lead like a legend. Each pillar serves as a cornerstone, providing a robust framework for gritty leadership that's both dynamic and sustainable. The integration of these four elements will elevate your capacity to lead effectively, turning you not just into a leader, but a legend in your field.

Hunt or Be Hunted

Grit isn't just a concept; it's a fusion of behavioral, emotional, and cognitive forces that can absolutely be cultivated. Can we master our behaviors? Unquestionably. Can we harness our emotions and adapt them to serve us, even in the face of overwhelming odds? Without a doubt. Is our thinking malleable, sculpted by the incredible power of neuroplasticity? Absolutely. This means that grit isn't a gift bestowed upon a fortunate few. It's a skill, a mindset, a set of behaviors, and a life philosophy that can be developed in anyone. And once honed, it transforms you into a legend in leadership.

So as you stand at the crossroads, remember this: hunt or be hunted. The choice is yours. If you're not actively hunting—pursuing growth, catalyzing innovation, and driving relentless success—you're already someone else's prey. Embrace the relentless pursuit of growth, innovation, and success. In the realm of leadership, those who do not seize opportunities and develop their grit defined by the Global G.R.I.T. System™ will inevitably become the prey. So adopt the Global G.R.I.T. System™ and become the hunter, not the hunted. The arena of leadership is unforgiving to those who don't seize their destiny. In the end, your choices are stark yet infinitely empowering: hunt or be hunted.

Know this—by choosing not to hunt, you've already become the hunted. So I extend an invitation to you. Come join me in the tall, wavering grass, the realm of the lioness—vigilant, patient, and utterly focused. Here I sit, executing, evaluating, influencing, owning, and ready to leap into the next chapter of destiny that awaits.

Let's make our move.

Let's go hunt.

"In the theater of life, you're either the scriptwriter, the director, or merely a character written in by circumstance. Choose to be the legend that writes its own lines, directs its own scenes, and above all, chooses to hunt—never to be hunted. This is how you lead, this is how you develop unbreakable grit. Seize your destiny and make your mark indelible. For in the end, legends aren't born, they're built."

Lara Jones

10 Key Leadership Lessons From This Chapter:

- The Global G.R.I.T. System™ is not a menu to choose from; it's a recipe to follow.

- Continuous training is essential, not optional. The Global G.R.I.T. System™ shapes performance, team dynamics, and talent strategies, requiring ongoing refreshers to elevate grit in all four pillars.

- The Global G.R.I.T. System™ isn't just a tool for development, it's a dynamic framework for sustained excellence.

- Sustain and regularly assess your grit through the Global G.R.I.T. System™ for dynamic, long-term excellence.

- For transformative leadership through the Global G.R.I.T. System™, begin with targeted training, foster early adoption among key departments for trust, then fully implement to harvest a pervasive culture of excellence.

- The Global G.R.I.T. System™ is not just a one-off event but a cultural shift that will drive long-term performance.

- By creating a team with the grit elements from the Global G.R.I.T. System™, you are building a synergistic force that elevates organizational excellence and capability.

- To lead with grit is to lead with fortitude.

- Master all four pillars of grit to evolve from a leader to a legend, ensuring dynamic and sustainable impact.

- Legends aren't born, they're built.

CHAPTER 12

The Hunt Continues

"In the whispered winds and the strength of a lioness, Jack 'JJ' lives on, guiding us to embody relentless grit in the face of life's trials—showing us that true resilience is not merely surviving the storm, but harnessing its power to propel us forward."

Lara Jones

Your Legacy Awaits

Amidst life's darkest moments and indescribable pain, I found my own luminosity, a torch fueled by my darkest days, harnessing this indomitable grit, not just for me but for you and countless others. Like a lioness who thrives in both daylight and darkness, I've transformed adversity into strength, hardship into wisdom. It's through employing this revolutionary and transformative system of grit that I've illuminated my path and the path for you and many others. This isn't merely survival, it's a determined commitment to thrive and impact lives. My son's memory, Jack Jones, my little JJ, and the future of my living children, not only endure but serve as a driving force for the indelible impact I aim to create on your life, and on the lives of countless others. I've taken the most excruciating chapters of my story and, guided by Jack's spirit, transmuted them into a legacy of resilience, purpose, and transformation. This is more than just coping—it's about rising, conquering, and leading. With every workshop I deliver, every keynote speech I give, and every life I touch, his light shines brighter. Together, we will not only navigate the complexities and challenges of life, but we will also redefine what it means to truly live. Jack's legacy lives on through each life bettered, each leader created, and each victory achieved in the realm of grit. Together, in honor of Jack, and in honor of you, we brave the intricate maze of life's challenges and triumphs.

Blueprint for Adversity

Adversity drives me to embody the fierce resilience of a lioness, even when faced with seemingly insurmountable odds. By channeling this steadfast system of grit, known as the Global G.R.I.T. System™, I've built not only a toolkit for survival but a roadmap for thriving—a blueprint for turning obstacles into stepping stones to prepare you for when grit chooses you. This is more than a personal journey for you and for me, it's a collective expedition in which you are honoring your adversity by facing life's complexities with intense tenacity. Together, we navigate, conquer, and emerge stronger, proving that even in the darkest times, resilience shines the brightest.

Hunt or Be Hunted

So, hunt or be hunted. You decide. But know if you are not hunting, you are already being hunted. Make your decision, but know that inaction is a decision in itself. Are you ready? The grass is swaying, the moment is now, and destiny waits for no one. With eyes wide open and the Global G.R.I.T. System™ as your unbreakable compass, you're not just prepared to seize the opportunity—you're poised to define it.

**Let the hunt begin,
let the hunt continue, and
let your legend be written.**

Never give up.

*"In the wilds of life, let your grit
be the roar that silences doubt,
your spirit the lioness that never
ceases to hunt, and your journey
the unyielding pursuit that writes
the legend only you can own."*

Lara Jones

ABOUT THE AUTHOR

Lara Jones

Lara Jones is one of the most requested speakers on grit and is an award-winning Leadership Performance Expert, Keynote Speaker, Creator of the Global G.R.I.T. System™, Founder and CEO of two global businesses Be A Legend and G.R.I.T. Global™, accomplished author, athlete and executive coach. Originally from the UK, and now residing in Arizona, United States, she has a track record of skyrocketing companies into  multimillion-dollar empires. She has been crowned the WORLDWIDE STEVIE® Award Winner for "Woman of the Year," "Female Entrepreneur of the Year," "Female Executive of the Year," and "Best Female Thought Leader of the Year" for her creation of the Global G.R.I.T. System™, including the Grit Type Indicator™. Lara has worked with Fortune 100 and 500 companies, US military, celebrities, and executives to develop and enhance performance on multiple levels for leaders, teams, and entire organizations. Lara has been featured on numerous podcasts, worked with and spoken in front of many well known household names including Goldman Sachs, Wells Fargo, KPMG, Northwestern Mutual, Schlumberger and more. Lara has been featured by PBS Brainline for her grit and resilience facing the loss of her youngest son and nearly her own life. As the renowned Grit Girl™, Lara has channeled her deep expertise and research into creating the Global G.R.I.T. System™ that is unveiled in this book. This innovative and tailored framework identifies the four pillars and "types" of grit, accompanied by a bespoke adoption process that transforms theory into action, creating a bespoke quadrant for grit. Lara guides you in both identifying your grit strengths through the Grit Type Indicator™ and honing your abilities across all dimensions of grit to achieve peak performance and unparalleled excellence through her proprietary Global G.R.I.T. System™. Lara is a wife to a US Marine and mother to her children, while also serving on the advisory board for Warrior Rising, a national non-profit organization helping veterans transition from military to entrepreneurship. She also sits on the committee for Dignity Health's Foundation "Heaven Hummingbirds," providing program development, emotional and psychological support for parents who have lost children through pregnancy and infant loss.

For Booking: www.larajones.com

Scan the QR code to get a sneak peek into your grit strength. See quick insights in just minutes.

www.larajones.com

REFERENCES BY CHAPTER

CHAPTER 1: Welcome to the Hunt

1   Yahya, J. (2021). Breaking Beyond the Borders of the Brain: Self-Control as a Situated Ability. *Front Psychol.*, 12(617434). 10.3389/fpsyg.2021.617434

2   Casagrande, M. (2022, October 17). *Saban says 'nobody is entitled to a position' as discipline troubles continue.* al.com: https://www.al.com/alabamafootball/2022/10/saban-says-nobody-is-entitled-to-a-position-as-discipline-troubles-continue.html

3   Steimer, T. (2002). The biology of fear and anxiety-related behaviors. *Dialogues Clin Neurosci.*, 4(3): 231–249. doi: 10.31887/DCNS.2002.4.3/tsteimer

4   Tugade, M.M. and Fredrickson, B.L. (2004). Resilient Individuals Use Positive Emotions to Bounce Back From Negative Emotional Experiences. *J Pers Soc Psychol.*, 86(2). 230-333. doi: 10.1037/0022-3514.86.2.320

5   Mobbs, D., Hagan, C.C., Dalgleish, T., Silston, B., and Prévost, C. (2015). The ecology of human fear: survival optimization and the nervous system. *Front Neurosci.*, 9(55). doi: 10.3389/fnins.2015.00055

6   Csikszentmihalyi, M. (1996) Creativity: Flow and the Psychology of discovery and intervention. Harper Perennial.

7   Park, D.C. (2013). The aging mind: neuroplasticity in response to cognitive training *Dialogues Clin Neurosci.*, 15(1): 109–119. doi: 10.31887/DCNS.2013.15.1/dpark

8   Kolb, B., & Gibb, R. (2011). Brain Plasticity and Behaviour in the Developing Brain *J Can Acad Child Adolesc Psychiatry*, 20(4): 265-276.

CHAPTER 2: The Birth of Grit

1   Monica Taylor-Desir. (2022, November). *What is Posttraumatic Stress Disorder (PTSD)?* American Psychiatric Association: https://www.psychiatry. org/patients-families/ptsd/what-is-ptsd#:~:text=PTSD%20affects%20 approximately%203.5%20percent,with%20PTSD%20in%20their%20lifetime.

CHAPTER 3: The Myths: What You Think You Know About Grit and Why You're Wrong (And Why It's Not Your Fault)

1   Schmidt, F. T. C., Fleckenstein, J., Retelsdorf, J., Eskreis-Winkler, L., & Möller, J. (2019). Measuring grit: A German validation and a domain-specific approach to grit. *European Journal of Psychological Assessment, 35*(3), 436–447.

2   Duckworth, A.L., Peterson, C., Matthews, M.D., Kelly, D.R. (2007). Grit: perseverance and passion for long-term goals. J Pers Soc Psychol., 92(6), 1087-101.

3   Bandura, A. (1977). Self-efficacy: toward a unifying theory of behavioral change. *Psychol Rev., 84,* 191-215.

4   Salles, A. Cohen, G.L., Mueller, C.M. (2013). The relationship between grit and resident well-being. *Am J Surg., 207*(2): 251-254.

5   Jachimowicz, J. M., Wihler, A., Bailey, E.R., & Galinsky, A.D. (2018). Why grit requires perseverance and passion to positively predict performance. *Proc Natl Acad Sci., 115* (40) 9980-9985. doi.org/10.1073/pnas.1803561115

6   Watson, N.F., Badr, M.S., Belenky, G., Bliwise, D.L., Buxton, O.M., Buysse, D., Dinges, D.F., Gangwisch, J., Grandner., M.A., Kushida, C., Malhotra, R.K., Martin, J.L., Patel, S.R., Quan, S.F., & Tasali, E. (2015). Recommended Amount of Sleep for a Healthy Adult: A Joint Consensus Statement of the American Academy of Sleep Medicine and Sleep Research Society. *Sleep, 38*(6):843-4. doi: 10.5665/sleep.4716. PMID: 26039963; PMCID: PMC4434546.

7   Kiecolt-Glaser, J.K. (2010) Stress, Food, and Inflammation: Psychoneuroimmunology and Nutrition at the Cutting Edge. Psychosom Med., 72(4), 365–369.

8   Briguglio, M., Vitale, J. A., Galentino, R., Banfi,G., Dina, C.Z., Bona, A., Panzica, G., Porta, M., Dell'Osso, B., & Glick, I.D. (2020) Healthy Eating, Physical Activity, and Sleep Hygiene (HEPAS) as the Winning Triad for Sustaining Physical and Mental Health in Patients at Risk for or with Neuropsychiatric Disorders: Considerations for Clinical Practice. *Neuropsychiatr Dis Treat., 16:* 55-70. doi: 10.2147/NDT.S229206

9 Mead, M.N. (2008). Benefits of Sunlight: A Bright Spot for Human Health. *Environ Health Perspect., 116*(4): 160-167.

10 Gonlepa, M.K, Dilawar S, Amosun, T.S. (2023). Understanding employee creativity from the perspectives of grit, work engagement, person organization fit, and feedback. *Front Psychol., 27*(13), doi: 10.3389/fpsyg. 2022.1012315

11 Engle-Friedman, M. (2014). The effects of sleep loss on capacity and effort. *Sleep Sci., 7*(4): 213-224.

12 Kiecolt-Glaser, J.K. (2010) Stress, Food, and Inflammation: Psychoneuroimmunology and Nutrition at the Cutting Edge. *Psychosom Med., 72*(4), 365-369.

13 Kolb, B., & Gibb, R. (2011). Brain Plasticity and Behaviour in the Developing Brain *J Can Acad Child Adolesc Psychiatry., 20*(4): 265-276.

14 Park, D.C. (2013). The aging mind: neuroplasticity in response to cognitive training *Dialogues Clin Neurosci., 15*(1): 109-119. doi: 10.31887/DCNS.2013. 15.1/dpark

CHAPTER 4: G.R.I.T. Through It™

1 Duckworth, A., Peterson, C., Matthews, M D., & Kelly, D. (2007). Grit: Perseverance and Passion for Long-Term Goals. *Journal of Personality and Social Psychology, 92*(6):1087-101 doi:10.1037/0022-3514.92.6.1087

2 Armstrong, K. (2019, October 29). *Carol Dweck on How Growth Mindsets Can Bear Fruit in the Classroom.* Association for Psychological Science. https://www.psychologicalscience.org/observer/dweck-growth-mindsets

3 Blackwell, L.S., Trzesniewski K.H., Dweck C.S. (2007). Implicit theories of intelligence predict achievement across an adolescent transition: A longitudinal study and an intervention. *Child Dev., 78*:246-263. doi: 10.1111/j.1467-8624.2007.00995.x

4 Hughes, B.L., Zaki J. (2015). The neuroscience of motivated cognition. *Trends Cogn. Sci., 19*:62-64. doi: 10.1016/j.tics.2014.12.006

5 Ng, B. (2018). The Neuroscience of Growth Mindset and Intrinsic Motivation. *Brain Sci., 8*(2): 20. doi: 10.3390/brainsci8020020

6 Rao, S.T.S., Asha, M.R., Rao, J, K.S., Vasudevaraju, P. (2009). The biochemistry of belief. *Indian J Psychiatry, 51*(4): 239-241. doi: 10.4103/0019-5545.58285

7   Rao, S.T.S., Asha, M.R., Rao, J, K.S., Vasudevaraju, P. (2009). The biochemistry of belief. *Indian J Psychiatry, 51*(4): 239–241. doi: 10.4103/0019-5545.58285

8   Ng, B. (2018). The Neuroscience of Growth Mindset and Intrinsic Motivation. *Brain Sci., 8*(2): 20. doi: 10.3390/brainsci8020020

CHAPTER 5: The Global G.R.I.T. System™

1   Vaish, A., Grossman, T., & Woodward, A. (2008). Not all emotions are created equal: The negativity bias in social-emotional development. *Psychol Bull., 134*(3): 383-403. doi: 10.1037/0033-2909.134.3.383

2   Soares, V.A., Hankonen, N., Presseau, J., Rodrigues, A., Sniehotta, F.F. (2018). Developing Behavior Change Interventions for Self-Management in Chronic Illness. *Eur Psychol.* 24(1): 7–25. doi: 10.1027/1016-9040/a000330

3   Crum, J. (2023). Understanding Mental Health and Cognitive Restructuring With Ecological Neuroscience. *Front Psychiatry, 12*:697095. doi: 10.3389/fpsyt.2021.697095

4   Leary, M.R. (2015). Emotional responses to interpersonal rejection. *Dialogues Clin Neurosci., 17*(4): 435-441. doi: 10.31887/DCNS.2015.17.4/mleary

5   Wang, K., Nickerson J. V. (2017). A literature review on individual creativity support systems. *Comput. Hum. Behav., 74:* 139-151. doi: 10.1016/j.chb.2017.04.035

6   Zhao, S., Jiang, Y., Peng, X., Hong J. (2021). Knowledge sharing direction and innovation performance in organizations. *Eur. J. Innov. Manag., 24:* 371-394. doi: 10.1108/EJIM-09-2019-0244

7   Ye, P., Liu, L., Tan, J. (2022). Influence of leadership empowering behavior on employee innovation behavior: The moderating effect of personal development support. *Front Psychol., 13*:1022377. doi: 10.3389/fpsyg.2022.1022377

8   Ye, P., Liu, L., Tan, J. (2022). Influence of leadership empowering behavior on employee innovation behavior: The moderating effect of personal development support. Front Psychol., 13:1022377. doi: 10.3389/fpsyg.2022.1022377

9   Kent, M. (2009, October 7). *Coke Didn't Make American Fat.* Wall Street Journal: https://www.wsj.com/articles/SB10001424052748703298004574455464120581696

10 Callahan, D. (2013). Obesity: Chasing an Elusive Epidemic. *Hastings Center Report, 43:* 34-40. doi: 10.1002/hast.114

11 Lozano, E.B (2019). The effect of admitting fault versus shifting blame on expectations for others to do the same. PLoS One, 14(3): e0213276. doi: 10.1371/journal.pone.0213276

12 Pickard, H. (2022). Responsibility without blame: Empathy and the effective treatment of personality disorder. *Neurosci Biobehav., 125:* 380-391. doi: 10.1353/ppp.2011.0032

13 Park, D., Tsukayama, E., Yu, A., & Duckworth, A. (2020). The development of grit and growth mindset during adolescence. *J Exp Child Psychol., 198:*104889. doi: 10.1016/j.jecp.2020.104889

14 Rao, S.T.S., Asha, M.R., Rao, J, K.S., Vasudevaraju, P. (2009). The biochemistry of belief. *Indian J Psychiatry., 51*(4): 239-241. doi: 10.4103/0019-5545.58285

15 Dweck, S., & Yeager, D. S. (2019). Mindsets: A view from two eras. *Perspect Psychol., 14*(3): 481-496. doi: 10.1177/1745691618804166

16 Romanelli, F., Bird, E., and Ryan, M. (2009). Learning Styles: A Review of Theory, Application, and Best Practices. *Am J Pharm Educ., 73*(1): 09. doi: 10.5688/aj730109

17 Felder, R.M. (1993). Reaching the second tier: learning and teaching styles in college science education. *J Coll Sci Teaching, 23:*286-90.

CHAPTER 6: Get it Done: The "G" in the Global G.R.I.T. System

1   Kennedy, D.R., and Porter, A. L. (2022). The Illusion of Urgency. *Am J Pharm Educ., 86*(7): 8914.

2   Liu, Q. & Tong, Y. (2022). Employee growth mindset and innovative behavior: The roles of employee strengths use and strengths-based leadership. *Front Psychol., 13:* 814154. doi: 10.3389/fpsyg.2022.814154

3   Gupta, M., & Sharma, A. (2021). Fear of missing out: A brief overview of origin, theoretical underpinnings and relationship with mental health. *World J Clin Cases, 9*(19): 4881-4889. doi: 10.12998/wjcc.v9.i19.4881

4   Zhu, M., Yang, Y., & Hsee, C. K. (2018). The mere urgency effect. Journal of Consumer Research, 45(3), 673-690.

5   Kennedy, D.R., and Porter, A. L. (2022). The Illusion of Urgency. *Am J Pharm Educ., 86*(7): 8914.

6   Fisk, S.R. (2020). Bold or reckless? The impact of workplace risk-taking on attributions and expected outcomes. PLoS One, 15(3). doi: 10.1371/journal.pone.0228672

7   Jung, C.C. (1976). *Psychological Types*. Volume 6: Princeton University Press

8   Budin, W.C. (2017). Building Confidence. *J Perinat Educ.,* 26(3): 107-109. doi: 10.1891/1058-1243.26.3.107

9   Bandura, A. (1986). Social foundations of thought and action: A social cognitive theory. Englewood Cliffs, NJ: Prentice-Hall

10 D'Souza, F., Egan, S.J., & Rees, C.S. (2011). The relationship between perfectionism, stress and burnout in clinical psychologists. *Behaviour Change,* 28(1):17-28. doi: 10.1375/bech.28.1.17.

11 Fisk, S.R. (2020). Bold or reckless? The impact of workplace risk-taking on attributions and expected outcomes. *PLoS One,* 15(3). doi: 10.1371/journal.pone.0228672

CHAPTER 7: Reframe Thinking:
The "R" in the Global G.R.I.T. System™

1   Chand, S.P., Kuckel, D.P., Huecker, M.R. (2023). *Cognitive behavior Therapy.* National Library of Medicine: StatPearls Publishing LLC. https://www.ncbi.nlm.nih.gov/books/NBK470241/

2   Vaish, A., Grossman, T., & Woodward, A. (2008). Not all emotions are created equal: The negativity bias in social-emotional development. *Psychol Bull.,* 134(3): 383-403. doi: 10.1037/0033-2909.134.3.383

3   Tseng, J., & Poppenk, J. (2020). Brain meta-state transitions demarcate thoughts across task contexts exposing the mental noise of trait neuroticism. *Nature Communications,* 11(1):3480. doi: 10.1038/s41467-020-17255-9.

4   Ehring, T,. & Watkins, E.R. (2008). Repetitive negative thinking as a transdiagnostic process. *Int J Cogn Ther.,* 1: 192-205

5   Hanson, R. & Mendius, R. (2009). *Buddha's Brain: The Practical Neuroscience of Happiness, Love & Wisdom.* Oakland, CA: New Harbinger Publications, Inc.

6   Corey, G. (2008). *Theory and practice of counseling and psychotherapy* (8th ed., pp. 273-295). Belmont, CA: Thomson Higher Education

7   Ellis, A. (1994). Post-traumatic stress disorder (PTSD): A rational emotive behavioral theory. *Journal of Rational-Emotive and Cognitive-Behavior Therapy, 12*(1): 3-25. doi.org/10.1007/BF02354487

8   Ellis, A. (1994). Post-traumatic stress disorder (PTSD): A rational emotive behavioral theory. *Journal of Rational-Emotive and Cognitive-Behavior Therapy, 12*(1): 3-25. doi.org/10.1007/BF02354487

9   Corey, G. (2008). *Theory and practice of counseling and psychotherapy* (8th ed., pp. 273-295). Belmont, CA: Thomson Higher Education

10   Ehlers, A. (2004). CBT of PTSD in Severe Mental Illness: A Promising Approach with possibilities for further development. *American Journal of Psychiatric Rehabilitation, 7*(2), 201-204. doi:10.1080/15487760490476237

11   Ehlers, A. (2004). CBT of PTSD in Severe Mental Illness: A Promising Approach with possibilities for further development. *American Journal of Psychiatric Rehabilitation, 7*(2), 201-204. doi:10.1080/15487760490476237

12   Burns, D.D. (2008). *Feeling Good: The New Mood Therapy.* New York, NY: Harper Collins.

13   Tseng, J., & Poppenk, J. (2020). Brain meta-state transitions demarcate thoughts across task contexts exposing the mental noise of trait neuroticism. *Nature Communications, 11*(1);3480. doi: 10.1038/s41467-020-17255-y.

14   Norris, C. (2021). The negativity bias, revisited: Evidence from neuroscience measures and an individual differences approach. *Soc Neurosci., 16*(1): 68-82. doi: 10.1080/17470919.2019.1696225

15   Hanson, R. & Mendius, R. (2009). Buddha's Brain: *The Practical Neuroscience of Happiness, Love & Wisdom.* Oakland, CA: New Harbinger Publications, Inc.

16   Singleton, S. (2017, May 25). *Carson knows that with the right mindset, anything is possible.* The Hill. https://thehill.com/blogs/pundits-blog/the-administration/335138-if-you-dont-have-the-mindset-to-believe-in-yourself-how/

17   Cassidy, J., Jones, J. D., & Shaver, P. R. (2013). Contributions of attachment theory and research: A framework of future research, translation, and policy. *Dev Psychopathol., 25*(4_0_2): 1415-1434. doi: 10.1017/S0954579413000692

18 Felix, S. (2016, June 27). *Universal grammar in language acquisition.* Cambridge University Press. https://www.cambridge.org/core/journals/canadian-journal-of-linguistics-revue-canadienne-de-linguistique/article/abs/universal-grammar-in-language-acquisition/FFFAA1F729C9CCA7E37AD8029A2B823E

19 Norris, C. (2021). The negativity bias, revisited: Evidence from neuroscience measures and an individual differences approach. *Soc Neurosci., 16*(1): 68-82. doi: 10.1080/17470919.2019.1696225

20 Hanson, R. & Mendius, R. (2009). *Buddha's Brain: The Practical Neuroscience of Happiness, Love & Wisdom.* Oakland, CA: New Harbinger Publications, Inc.

21 Fredrickson, B. L. (2001). The role of positive emotions in positive psychology: The broaden-and-build theory of positive emotions. *American Psychologist, 56*(3), 218-226

22 Fredrickson, B. L. (2001). The role of positive emotions in positive psychology: The broaden-and-build theory of positive emotions. *American Psychologist, 56*(3), 218-226

23 Kennedy, M.B. (2021). Synaptic Signaling in Learning and Memory. *Cold Spring Harb Perspect Biol, 8*(2): a016824

24 Fredrickson, B. L. (2001). The role of positive emotions in positive psychology: The broaden-and-build theory of positive emotions. *American Psychologist, 56*(3), 218-226

25 Hanson, R. & Mendius, R. (2009). *Buddha's Brain: The Practical Neuroscience of Happiness, Love & Wisdom.* Oakland, CA: New Harbinger Publications, Inc.

26 Fredrickson, B. L. (2004). The broaden-and-build theory of positive emotions. *Philos Trans R Soc Lond B Biol Sci., 359*(1449): 1367-1378. doi: 10.1098/rstb.2004.1512

27 Jung, C.C. (1976). *Psychological Types.* Volume 6: Princeton University Press

28 Tseng, J. & Poppenk, J. (2020). Brain meta-state transitions demarcate thoughts across task contexts exposing the mental noise of trait neuroticism. *Nature Communications, 11*(1):3480. doi: 10.1038/s41467-020-17255-9.

29 Ehring, T,. & Watkins, E.R. (2008). Repetitive negative thinking as a transdiagnostic process. *Int J Cogn Ther., 1:* 192-205

30   Fredrickson, B. L. (2001). The role of positive emotions in positive psychology: The broaden-and-build theory of positive emotions. *American Psychologist, 56*(3), 218-226

31   Wason, P.C. (1960). On the failure to eliminate hypotheses in a conceptual task. *Quarterly Journal of Experimental Psychology, 12*(3):129-140. doi.org/10.1080/17470216008416717

32   Norris, C. (2021). The negativity bias, revisited: Evidence from neuroscience measures and an individual differences approach. *Soc Neurosci., 16*(1): 68-82. doi: 10.1080/17470919.2019.1696225

33   Smith, G. K., Mills, C, Paxton, A., and Christoff, K. (2018). Mind-wandering rates fluctuate across the day: evidence from an experience-sampling study. *Cogn Res Princ Implic., 3*(1):54. doi: 10.1186/s41235-018-0141-4.

34   Smith, G. K., Mills, C, Paxton, A., and Christoff, K. (2018). Mind-wandering rates fluctuate across the day: evidence from an experience-sampling study. *Cogn Res Princ Implic., 3*(1):54. doi: 10.1186/s41235-018-0141-4.

Chapter 8: Impact Others: The "I" in the Global G.R.I.T. System™

1   Opoku, M., Choi, S., Kang, S. (2019). Servant Leadership and Innovative Behaviour: An Empirical Analysis of Ghana's Manufacturing Sector. *Sustainability, 11*:6273. doi. 10.3390/su11226273.

2   Ye, P., Liu, L., Tan, J. (2022). Influence of leadership empowering behavior on employee innovation behavior: The moderating effect of personal development support. Front Psychol, 13:1022377. doi: 10.3389/fpsyg.2022.1022377

3   Opoku, M., Choi, S., Kang, S. (2019). Servant Leadership and Innovative Behaviour: An Empirical Analysis of Ghana's Manufacturing Sector. *Sustainability, 11*:6273. doi: 10.3390/su11226273.

4   Opoku, M., Choi, S., Kang, S. (2019). Servant Leadership and Innovative Behaviour: An Empirical Analysis of Ghana's Manufacturing Sector. *Sustainability, 11*:6273. doi: 10.3390/su11226273.

5   Pervaiz, S, Li, G, & He, Q. (2021). The mechanism of goal-setting participation's impact on employees' proactive behavior, moderated mediation role of power distance. *PLoS One., 16*(12):e0260625. doi: 10.1371/journal.pone.0260625.

6   Cai, W., Khapova, S., Bossink, B., Lysova, E., & Yuan, J. (2020). Optimizing Employee Creativity in the Digital Era: Uncovering the Interactional Effects of Abilities, Motivations, and Opportunities. *Int J Environ Res Public Health, 17*(3):1038. doi: 10.3390/ijerph17031038.

7   Ye, P., Liu, L., Tan, J. (2022). Influence of leadership empowering behavior on employee innovation behavior: The moderating effect of personal development support. *Front Psychol, 13*:1022377. doi: 10.3389/fpsyg.2022. 1022377

8   Yan, Y., Zhang, J., Akhtar, M.N., & Liang, S. (2023). Positive leadership and employee engagement: The roles of state positive affect and individualism-collectivism. *Curr Psychol.* 42(11):9109-9118. doi: 10.1007/s12144-021-02192-7.

9   Seppälä, E., & Cameron, K. (2022, April 18). *The Best Leaders Have a Contagious Positive Energy.* Harvard Business Review: https://hbr.org/2022/04/the-best-leaders-have-a-contagious-positive-energy

10   Laguna, M., Walachowska, K., Gorgievski-Duijvesteijn, M.J., & Moriano, J.A. (2019). Authentic Leadership and Employees' Innovative Behaviour: A Multilevel Investigation in Three Countries. *Int J Environ Res Public Health, 16*(21):4201. doi: 10.3390/ijerph16214201.

11   Cavaness, K., Picchioni, A., & Fleshman, J.W. (2020). Linking Emotional Intelligence to Successful Health Care Leadership: The Big Five Model of Personality. *Clin Colon Rectal Surg.* 33(4):195-203. doi: 10.1055/s-0040-1709435.

12   Hamel, G., Doz, Y., & Prahalad, C.K. (1989, January-February). *Collaborate with Your Competitors—and Win.* Harvard Business Review: https://hbr.org/1989/01/collaborate-with-your-competitors-and-win

13   Johannsen, R., & Zak, P.J. (2020). Autonomy Raises Productivity: An Experiment Measuring Neurophysiology. *Front Psychol.* 15(11):963. doi: 10.3389/fpsyg.2020.00963.

14   Poindexter, W. & Craig, J. (2022, October 19). *Survey: What Attracts Top Tech Talent?* Harvard Business Review: https://hbr.org/2022/10/survey-what-attracts-top-tech-talent

15   Gorzelany, J., Gorzelany-Dziadkowiec, M., Luty, L., Firlej, K., Gaisch, M., Dudziak, O., & Scott, C. (2021). Finding links between organisation's culture and innovation. The impact of organisational culture on university innovativeness. *PLoS One, 16*(10):e0257962. doi: 10.1371/journal.pone.0257962.

16 Vo, T,T,D., Tuliao, K.V., & Chen, C.W. (2022). Work Motivation: The Roles of Individual Needs and Social Conditions. *Behav Sci (Basel), 12*(2):49. doi: 10.3390/bs12020049.

17 Duarte, A.P., Ribeiro, N., Semedo, A.S., & Gomes DR. (2021). Authentic Leadership and Improved Individual Performance: Affective Commitment and Individual Creativity's Sequential Mediation. *Front Psychol,. 7*;12:675749. doi: 10.3389/fpsyg.2021.675749.

18 Opoku, M., Choi, S., Kang, S. (2019). Servant Leadership and Innovative Behaviour: An Empirical Analysis of Ghana's Manufacturing Sector. *Sustainability, 11*:6273. doi: 10.3390/su11226273.

19 Okello, D.R., & Gilson, L. (2015). Exploring the influence of trust relationships on motivation in the health sector: a systematic review. *Hum Resour Health., 13*:16. doi: 10.1186/s12960-015-0007-5.

20 Opoku, M., Choi, S., Kang, S. (2019). Servant Leadership and Innovative Behaviour: An Empirical Analysis of Ghana's Manufacturing Sector. *Sustainability, 11*:6273. doi: 10.3390/su11226273.

21 Rahmadani, V.G., Schaufeli, W.B., Stouten, J., Zhang, Z., & Zulkarnain, Z. (2020). Engaging Leadership and Its Implication for Work Engagement and Job Outcomes at the Individual and Team Level: A Multi-Level Longitudinal Study. *Int J Environ Res Public Health, 17*(3):776. doi: 10.3390/ijerph17030776.

22 Ye, P., Liu, L., Tan, J. (2022). Influence of leadership empowering behavior on employee innovation behavior: The moderating effect of personal development support. *Front Psychol, 13*:1022377. doi: 10.3389/fpsyg.2022.1022377

23 Kuyatt, A. (2011). Managing for Innovation: Reducing the Fear of Failure. *Journal of Strategic Leadership, 2*(3). https://www.regent.edu/journal/journal-of-strategic-leadership/managing-change-and-innovation/

24 Festinger, L. (1954). A theory of social comparison process. *Human Relations, 7*(2): 117- 140. doi.org/10.1177/001872675400700202

25 Rahmadani, V.G., Schaufeli, W.B., Stouten, J., Zhang, Z., & Zulkarnain, Z. (2020). Engaging Leadership and Its Implication for Work Engagement and Job Outcomes at the Individual and Team Level: A Multi-Level Longitudinal Study. *Int J Environ Res Public Health. 17*(3):776. doi: 10.3390/ijerph17030776.

CHAPTER 9: Take Responsibility:
The "T" in the Global G.R.I.T. System™

1   Parker, J., & Davies, B. (2020). No Blame No Gain? From a No Blame Culture to a Responsibility Culture in Medicine. *J Appl Philos, 37*(4): 646-660. doi: 10.1111/japp.12433

2   Goodin, R.E. (1987) 'Apportioning responsibilities'. *Law and Philosophy 6, 2*(1987): 167-85.

3   Grotberg, E. H. (1999). *How to deal with anything.* New York: MJF Books.

4   Norris, C. (2021). The negativity bias, revisited: Evidence from neuroscience measures and an individual differences approach. *Soc Neurosci., 16*(1): 68-82. doi: 10.1080/17470919.2019.1696225

5   Iqbal, S., Farid, T., Khan, M.K., Zhang, Q., Khattak, A., & Ma, J. (2019). Bridging the Gap between Authentic Leadership and Employees Communal Relationships through Trust. *Int J Environ Res Public Health. 30;*17(1):250. doi: 10.3390/ijerph17010250.

6   Ronquillo, Y., Ellis, V.L., & Toney-Butler, T.J. (2023). *Conflict Management.* National Library of Medicine. Treasure Island (FL): StatPearls Publishing. https://www.ncbi.nlm.nih.gov/books/NBK470432/

7   Li, M., Yang, F., & Akhtar, M. W. (2022). Responsible Leadership Effect on Career Success: The Role of Work Engagement and Self-Enhancement Motives in the Education Sector. *Front Psychol., 13.* doi.org/10.3389/fpsyg. 2022.888386

8   Coleman, J. (2012, August 30). *Take Ownership of Your Actions by Taking Responsibility.* Harvard Business Review: https://hbr.org/2012/08/take-ownership-of-your-actions

9   Zhou, Q., Mao, J.Y., Tang, F. (2020). Don't Be Afraid to Fail Because You Can Learn From It! How Intrinsic Motivation Leads to Enhanced Self-Development and Benevolent Leadership as a Boundary Condition. *Front Psychol., 16;* 11:699. doi: 10.3389/fpsyg.2020.00699.

10   Liang, TP., Li, Y.W., & Yen, N.S. (2021). Framing and self-responsibility modulate brain activities in decision escalation. *BMC Neurosci., 22,*(19). doi: Doi.org/10.1186/s12868-021-00625-4

11   Coleman, J. (August 30, 2012). Take Ownership of Your Actions by Taking Responsibility. Harvard Business Review: https://hbr.org/2012/08/take-ownership-of-your-actions

12   Hofmann, S.G., & Hay, A.C. (2018). Rethinking avoidance: Toward a balanced approach to avoidance in treating anxiety disorders. *J Anxiety Disord., 55:*14-21. doi: 10.1016/j.janxdis.2018.03.004

13   Lin, M., Ling, Q. (2016). Evaluation and enlightenment of empowering leadership research. J. *Account. Econ., 4:* 111–119. doi: 10.13504/j.cnki. Issn1008-2700.2016.04.015

14   Grotberg, E. H. (1999). *How to deal with anything.* New York: MJF Books.

15   Grotberg, E. H. (1999). *How to deal with anything.* New York: MJF Books.

16   Smith, S. (2019, October 24). *Lack of Trust Can Make Workplaces Sick and Dysfunctional.* Forbes: https://www.forbes.com/sites/forbescoachescouncil/2019/10/24/lack-of-trust-can-make-workplaces-sick-and-dysfunctional/?sh=3bc8b07144d1

17   Smith, S. (2019, October 24). *Lack of Trust Can Make Workplaces Sick and Dysfunctional.* Forbes: https://www.forbes.com/sites/forbescoachescouncil/2019/10/24/lack-of-trust-can-make-workplaces-sick-and-dysfunctional/?sh=3bc8b07144d1

18   Smith, S. (2019, October 24). *Lack of Trust Can Make Workplaces Sick and Dysfunctional.* Forbes: https://www.forbes.com/sites/forbescoachescouncil/2019/10/24/lack-of-trust-can-make-workplaces-sick-and-dysfunctional/?sh=3bc8b07144d1

19   King, R. (2013, February 28). *Groupon CEO fired; takes responsibility for company's poor performance.* ZDNet. https://www.zdnet.com/article/groupon-ceo-fired-takes-responsibility-for-companys-poor-performance/)

20   Bran, A., & Vaidis, D.C. (2020). On the Characteristics of the Cognitive Dissonance State: Exploration Within the Pleasure Arousal Dominance Model. *Psychol Belg., 60*(1):86-102. doi: 10.5334/pb.517.

21   Sutherland, L.A., Beavers, D.P., Kupper, L.L., Bernhardt, A.M., Heatherton, T. & Dalton, M.A. (2008). Like parent, like child: child food and beverage choices during role playing. *Arch Pediatr Adolesc Med., 162*(11):1063-9. doi: 10.1001/archpedi.162.11.1063.

22   Farson, R., & Keyes, R. (2002, August). *The Failure-Tolerant Leader.* Harvard Business Review: https://hbr.org/2002/08/the-failure-tolerant-leader

23 Zhou, Q., Mao, J.Y., Tang, F. (2020). Don't Be Afraid to Fail Because You Can Learn From It! How Intrinsic Motivation Leads to Enhanced Self-Development and Benevolent Leadership as a Boundary Condition. *Front Psychol., 16;* 11:699. doi: 10.3389/fpsyg.2020.00699.

24 Mirzadegan, J. (2023, July 10). Co-founder and CEO Rubrik, Bipul Sinha: Authenticity Reigns (146). *Grit.* Kleiner Perkins. https://podcasts.apple.com/no/podcast/co-founder-and-ceo-rubrik-bipul-sinha-authenticity-reigns/id1510985491?i=1000620475039

1 Nicholson, N. (1998, July-August). *How Hardwired is Human Behavior?* Harvard Business Review: https://hbr.org/1998/07/how-hardwired-is-human-behavior

CHAPTER 10: The Application of the Global G.R.I.T. System™

2 Blumberg, M.S. (2017). Development evolving: the origins and meanings of instinct. *Wiley Interdiscip Rev Cogn Sci., 8*(1-2):10.1002/wcs.1371. doi: 10.1002/wcs.1371

3 West-Eberhard, M.J. (2003). *Developmental plasticity and evolution.* Oxford University Press: New York.

4 Gustavson, D.E., Miyake, A., Hewitt, J.K., & Friedman, N.P. (2014). Genetic relations among procrastination, impulsivity, and goal-management ability: implications for the evolutionary origin of procrastination. *Psychol Sci., 25*(6):1178-88. doi: 10.1177/0956797614526260.

5 Gustavson, D.E., Miyake, A., Hewitt, J.K., & Friedman, N.P. (2014). Genetic relations among procrastination, impulsivity, and goal-management ability: implications for the evolutionary origin of procrastination. *Psychol Sci., 25*(6):1178-88. doi: 10.1177/0956797614526260.

6 Pervaiz, S., Li, G., & He, Q. (2021). The mechanism of goal-setting participation's impact on employees' proactive behavior, moderated mediation role of power distance. *PLoS One., 16*(12):e0260625. doi: 10.1371/journal.pone.0260625.

7 McEwen, B.S. (2012). Brain on stress: how the social environment gets under the skin. *Proc Natl Acad Sci., U S A. 16*:109(Suppl 2): 17180-17185. doi: 10.1073/pnas.1121254109

8 McEwen, B.S. (2012). Brain on stress: how the social environment gets under the skin. *Proc Natl Acad Sci., U S A. 16*:109(Suppl 2): 17180-17185. doi: 10.1073/pnas.1121254109

9   McEwen, B.S. (2012). Brain on stress: how the social environment gets under the skin. *Proc Natl Acad Sci., U S A. 16:*109(Suppl 2): 17180–17185. doi: 10.1073/pnas.1121254109

10   Ladouceur, C.D., Schlund, M.W., & Segreti, A.M. (2018). Positive reinforcement modulates fronto-limbic systems subserving emotional interference in adolescents. *Behav Brain Res., 15;*338:109-117. doi: 10.1016/j. bbr.2017.10.019.

11   Zhenjing, G., Chupradit, S., Ku, K.Y., Nassani, A.A., & Haffar, M. (2022). Impact of Employees' Workplace Environment on Employees' Performance: A Multi-Mediation Model. *Front Public Health, 13:*10:890400. doi: 10.3389/ fpubh.2022.890400.

12   Jarczok, M.N., Jarczok, M., Mauss, D., Koenig, J., Li, J., Herr, R.M., & Thayer, J.F. (2013) . Autonomic nervous system activity and workplace stressors-a systematic review. *Neurosci Biobehav Rev., 37*(8):1810-23. doi: 10.1016/j. neubiorev.2013.07.004.

13   Kolb, P. (2015, November 24). *How Michael Jordan's mindset made him a great competitor.* USA Basketball: https://www.usab.com/news/2015/11/ how-michael-jordans-mindset-made-him-a-great-competitor

14   Gopalkrishnan, N. (2018). Cultural Diversity and Mental Health: Considerations for Policy and Practice *Front Public Health., 19*(6):179. doi: 10.3389/fpubh.2018.00179.

15   Ackerman, S. (1992). *Discovering the Brain.* Washington (DC): National Academies Press (US): 2, Major Structures and Functions of the Brain: https:// www.ncbi.nlm.nih.gov/books/NBK234157/

16   Norris, C. (2021). The negativity bias, revisited: Evidence from neuroscience measures and an individual differences approach. *Soc Neurosci, 16*(1): 68-82. doi: 10.1080/17470919.2019.1696225

17   Miller, F.E. (2001). Challenging and changing stress-producing thinking. *West J Med., 174*(1):49-50. doi: 10.1136/ewjm.174.1.49.

18   McEwen, B.S. (2012). Brain on stress: how the social environment gets under the skin. *Proc Natl Acad Sci., U S A. 16:*109(Suppl 2): 17180–17185. doi: 10.1073/pnas.1121254109

19   McEwen, B.S. (2012). Brain on stress: how the social environment gets under the skin. *Proc Natl Acad Sci., U S A. 16:*109(Suppl 2): 17180–17185. doi: 10.1073/pnas.1121254109

20 Ganzel, B.L., Morris, P.A., & Wethington, E. (2010). Allostasis and the human brain: Integrating models of stress from the social and life sciences. *Psychol Rev., 117*:134-174.

21 Kadović, M., Mikšić, Š., & Lovrić, R. (2022). Ability of Emotional Regulation and Control as a Stress Predictor in Healthcare Professionals. *Int J Environ Res Public Health. 20*(1):541. doi: 10.3390/ijerph20010541.

22 Miller, F.E. (2001). Challenging and changing stress-producing thinking. *West J Med., 174*(1):49-50. doi: 10.1136/ewjm.174.1.49.

23 Fassbinder, E., Schweiger, U., Martius, D., Brand-de Wilde, O., & Arntz, A. (2016). Emotion Regulation in Schema Therapy and Dialectical Behavior Therapy. *Front Psychol., 14*:7(1373). doi: 10.3389/fpsyg.2016.01373.

24 Cooke, J. (2017, March 15). *Own your Happyness: A Q&A with Chris Gardner.* Forbes: https://www.forbes.com/sites/jaynacooke/2017/03/15/own-your-happyness-a-qa-with-chris-gardner/?sh=253696961b27

25 Oleynick, V.C., Thrash, T.M., LeFew, M.C., Moldovan, E.G., & Kieffaber PD. (2014). The scientific study of inspiration in the creative process: challenges and opportunities. *Front Hum Neurosci., 25*(8):436. doi: 10.3389/fnhum.2014.00436.

26 Park, S.Q., Kahnt, T., Dogan, A., Strang, S., Fehr, E., & Tobler, P.N. (2017). A neural link between generosity and happiness. *Nat Commun., 8*:15964. doi: 10.1038/ncomms15964.

27 Park, S.Q., Kahnt, T., Dogan, A., Strang, S., Fehr, E., & Tobler, P.N. (2017). A neural link between generosity and happiness. Nat Commun., 8:15964. doi: 10.1038/ncomms15964.

28 Schmutz, J.B., Meier, L.L., & Manser, T. (2019). How effective is teamwork really? The relationship between teamwork and performance in healthcare teams: a systematic review and meta-analysis. *BMJ Open., 9*(9):e028280. doi: 10.1136/bmjopen-2018-028280.

29 Müller, J.W. (2021). Education and inspirational intuition - Drivers of innovation. *Heliyon., 7*(9):e07923. doi: 10.1016/j.heliyon.2021.e07923.

30 Wan, X., He, R., Zhang, G., & Zhou, J. (2022). Employee engagement and open service innovation: The roles of creative self-efficacy and employee innovative behaviour. *Front Psychol., 13*:921687. doi: 10.3389/fpsyg.2022.921687.

31 Isaacson, W. (2012, April). *The Real Leadership Lessons of Steve Jobs*. Harvard Business Review: https://hbr.org/2012/04/the-real-leadership-lessons-of-steve-jobs

32 Thomas, A. (2016, July 20). *This Leadership Quality Was The Real Reason Steve Jobs Was a Success*. Inc: https://www.inc.com/andrew-thomas/why-steve-jobs-success-goes-far-deeper-than-vision-and-smarts.html

33 Lewis, A. 2022, October 26). *Good Leadership? It All Starts With Trust*. Harvard Business Publishing: https://www.harvardbusiness.org/good-leadership-it-all-starts-with-trust/

34 Mazzetti, G., & Schaufeli, W.B. (2022). The impact of engaging leadership on employee engagement and team effectiveness: A longitudinal, multi-level study on the mediating role of personal- and team resources. *PLoS One.*, *17*(6):e0269433. doi: 10.1371/journal.pone.0269433.

35 King, R. (2013, February 28). *Groupon CEO fired; takes responsibility for company's poor performance*. ZDNet. https://www.zdnet.com/article/groupon-ceo-fired-takes-responsibility-for-companys-poor-performance/)

36 Hougaard, R., & Carter, J. (2018, November 6). *Ego is the Enemy of Good Leadership*. Harvard Business Review: https://hbr.org/2018/11/ego-is-the-enemy-of-good-leadersh

37 Kolzow, D.R. (2014). *Leading from Within: Building Organizational Leadership Capacity*. International Economic Development Council: https://www.iedconline.org/clientuploads/Downloads/edrp/Leading_from_Within.pdf

38 Roth, P. (2022). How social context impacts the emergence of leadership structures. *Leadership*, *18*(4), 539–562. https://doi.org/10.1177/17427150221090375

39 Cavaness, K., Picchioni, A., & Fleshman, J.W. (2020). Linking Emotional Intelligence to Successful Health Care Leadership: The Big Five Model of Personality. *Clin Colon Rectal Surg.*, *33*(4):195-203. doi: 10.1055/s-0040-1709435.

40 Wilkins, C.H. (2018). Effective Engagement Requires Trust and Being Trustworthy. *Med Care, 56*(10 Suppl 1): S6–S8. doi: 10.1097/MLR.0000000000000953.

41 Steinmann, B., Klug, H.J.P., & Maier, G.W. (2018). The Path Is the Goal: How Transformational Leaders Enhance Followers' Job Attitudes and Proactive Behavior. *Front Psychol.*, *9*:2338. doi: 10.3389/fpsyg.2018.02338.

42 Neely, M.E. (1982). *The Abraham Lincoln Encyclopedia*. New York: Da Capo Press, Inc.

43 Lincoln, A. (1863). Gettysburg address delivered at Gettysburg Pa. Nov. 19th, . n. p. n. d. [Pdf] Retrieved from the Library of Congress, https://www.loc.gov/item/rbpe.24404500/.

44 Hobson, N. (2023, April 19). *25 Years Ago, Steve Jobs Saved Apple From Collapse*. Inc: https://www.inc.com/nick-hobson/25-years-ago-steve-jobs-saved-apple-from-collapse-its-a-lesson-for-every-tech-ceo-today.html

45 Shontell, A. (2010, October 26). *The Greatest Comeback Story Of All Time: How Apple Went From Near Bankruptcy To Billions In 13 Years*. Business Insider: https://www.businessinsider.com/apple-comeback-story-2010-10

46 Hobson, N. (2023, April 19). *25 Years Ago, Steve Jobs Saved Apple From Collapse*. Inc: https://www.inc.com/nick-hobson/25-years-ago-steve-jobs-saved-apple-from-collapse-its-a-lesson-for-every-tech-ceo-today.html

47 Laricchia, F. (2023, August 28). *Leading Tech Companies Worldwide 2023, by Market Cap*. Statista: https://www.statista.com/statistics/1350976/leading-tech-companies-worldwide-by-market-cap/#:~:text=As%20of%20August%202023%2C%20Apple,U.S.%20dollars%20in%20market%20capitalization.

48 Aydin, R. (2019, September 20). *How 3 guys turned renting air mattresses in their apartment into a $31 billion company, Airbnb*. Business Insider: https://www.businessinsider.com/how-airbnb-was-founded-a-visual-history-2016-2

CHAPTER 11: Commissioning the Global G.R.I.T. System™

1 Kim-Cohen J., & Turkewitz R. (2012). Resilience and measured gene-environment interactions. *Development and Psychopathology*, 24:1297–1306.

2 Newman, R. (2005). APA's Resilience Initiative. *Professional Psychology Research and Practice* 36(3):227-229

Made in the USA
Las Vegas, NV
14 November 2023

80840682R00116